Invisible

Invisible
Fiction but Painfully True

Angela Evans

Grateful Steps
Asheville, North Carolina

Grateful Steps Foundation
Crest Mountain
30 Ben Lippen School Road #107
Asheville, North Carolina 28806

Copyright © 2019 by Angela Evans
Library of Congress Control Number 2018913567

Evans, Angela
Invisible: Fiction but Painfully True

Illustrator Kirby Marion
ISBN 978-1-945714-19-1 Paperback

Printed in the United States of America
at Lightning Source
FIRST EDITION

All rights reserved. No part of this book
may be reproduced in any manner whatsoever
without written permission from the author.

www.gratefulsteps.org

To my brother Kirby. You put the truth in my fiction. Love you forever.

Contents

DEDICATION

PROLOGUE

1. THE BEGINNING
2. THE CHAOS STARTS
3. PROGRESSION
4. SPIRALING OUT OF CONTROL
5. THE SO-CALLED GOOD YEARS
6. NO MORE DENIAL
7. THE PROGRAM
8. A POSITIVE
9. HOME SWEET HOME
10. HEALED (NOT)
11. SATURATED
12. WORDS CAN HURT
13. REPEAT
14. SADNESS
15. STILL OBSESSED
16. CHANGES
17. NEW LIFE
18. BABIES AND MARRIAGE
19. LAST TRIP TO THE BEACH
20. A NEW HURT
21. ENDINGS ARE SAD
22. AN ADVENTURE END
23. THE END
24. ACCEPTANCE

EPILOGUE

I will be skinny. Next year when I come back to school, I will not be fat, and these people will not torture me, Derrick thought as he sat on the bus the last day of school.

Prologue

Every school day for the past year I was bullied from the moment I climbed on the bus. Kids made endless taunts and cruel comments. Most of the time they were just verbal abuse, but as I think about it, some were physical, like the time my shirt got ripped just because it was new. It was as if the bullies knew I was proud of it, and they wanted to take it from me. Or the time I had a hair style I really liked and they messed it up before school just to take away any confidence that I tried to muster. The spitting was bad too. The verbal taunts went on and on and were targeted at my weight. I've taken it for too long. Now I've had enough!

As I walked home from the bus stop one day, I thought of ways to lose weight over the summer. *There has to be a way for me to be skinny when I go back to school.* It would be my first year of high school and I knew I had the chance to make a new start. Middle school had been miserable and even though I liked the academics, I hated the other kids and the way they treated me.

    High school will be better, and I had the summer to make it work. I know I will have to starve, but it will be worth the effort. Not that I really want to be popular, I just don't want to be picked on anymore. When people say kids can be cruel, they do not truly know the extent that kids will go to when the victim is an outcast. They make it their life's work to make the outcast miserable. I had a few friends who tried to help me when they saw it happen, but they could not always be around, and I had to fend for myself. There was not a lot that they could do to fix the problem because it had gone on too long. I was now the target of *multiple* bullies, and it was not going to stop just because my friends defended me. It would take more than that to make them go away. My nephew and a few other people on the bus stood up for me, but they did not catch all the bullying. I hated to involve them; I did not want them to be a target as well, so I told them it was fine.

    When I walked in that day after school, my mom asked me about my day and I said that it was fine. I did not want to tell her what had really happened. She would only worry and call the school. Most of the teachers took the side of the bullies because those kids were athletic and popular. So calling the school was a waste of time and made it worse. Besides, school was over for the summer, and next year was going to be different.

* * *

I will not have to come in feeling this way ever again. I am going to be the one thing that I want the most next year. It is not skinny or popular; all I really want is to be invisible.

CHAPTER 1
Derrick

The Beginning

I DID IT. I am invisible. The person I was in middle school is gone. I lost seventy pounds over the summer and nobody even knows who I am. I even changed my hair, so nothing remains of my old self. My hair was brown and I wore it in an old school style, now it is blond and worn more like a hipster. I find it interesting that people do not even notice me now. On the bus this morning, I did not get the same taunts and bullying. They basically ignored me, which was the plan. I will ignore them and they will ignore me. I can live with the invisibility of it all.

I even had someone ask me in the hall if I was related to Derrick. I quickly said no and moved on. A part of me wanted to laugh in her face, it was so amusing to me. However, I do not want to be remembered. As far as I'm concerned the person that I was is dead. I will never be him again. I laughed and thought that maybe I should change my name too, but I knew it would be impossible without talking to my mom about everything, and that was not going to happen. I did not want her to know what I had been through. She would blame herself, and I refuse to allow her to suffer for one moment for all the bullies and assholes of the world.

The summer had been difficult. I went days without eating anything but an apple or two. I also tried to exercise, but that was difficult because I ate so little, and so my energy levels were low. The plan had worked. The starvation was worth every hunger pang. I left the old me behind. I will never be fat again. I cannot afford to be fat. I know I could not have survived the constant bullying for another year. I would not have lived through it mentally and physically. This was my only option.

There are people, like my sister, who are concerned with my weight loss. I keep reassuring her that I am fine. I just wanted to lose weight and I did. I had to work extra hard to hide things from her. She would pay attention and question my eating habits. Mom noticed too, but I told her it was just a diet and I would be fine. I exaggerated how much I was eating to her so that she would not worry. For the most part, I convinced her that I was eating more than enough. I am not sure my sister believed me because she also understands more than she lets on. She had heard about the bullying and wanted to put a stop to it. I wish I could make people understand that having your parents or relatives come to school and tattletale on the bully only makes it worse. Bullies say, "Snitches get stitches for a reason." The only solution would be to hire a bodyguard, but that was not going to happen either. This was the only way. Being skinny is the way to go, nobody notices me as much. I guess there is not as much of me to see. The irony of it does not escape me.

***

I am happy to have lost the weight, but I feel I need to lose more. A few more pounds and I will be satisfied. I just have to make myself stay away from food, which can be very challenging. I love food. The love of it is my dirty secret. At times it's almost unbearable to do without the one thing I love, the one thing that gives me pleasure. However, for the time being, food is my enemy, and I will not give in to my desire to eat. *Just a few more pounds.*

If a few more pounds will keep the bullies at bay, then I will do it without a second thought. I cannot have Sara come to school and defend me like she did when I was small. She always thought she had to be my champion, and she was good at the job.

I remember one time in first grade my teacher yelled at me and pointed her finger in my face. I just took it and did not say anything. I was too young to really understand that something could be done. One day my sister saw it, and after I got in the car, she questioned me about the teacher's behavior. When I told her that she did it all the time, Sara was livid. Sara is my protector because she is fifteen years older than I am.

"If she puts her finger in your face again, I will smack *her* face," she said and I smiled. I could not wait to go to school the next day and tell my teacher. When I told her what Sara said, she scowled at me but did not argue. When Sara arrived to pick me up, she ran out and questioned her. I knew Sara would not back down, so I waited for her response with excitement.

"Derrick told me that you said if I put my finger in his face again, you were going to smack me." She said it smugly and looked at me like I was a little liar.

Sara smiled sweetly at her and said, "That is exactly what I said and what I will do. I think it is wrong for a teacher to be a bully."

My teacher looked shocked and stalked off. She never put her finger in my face again, and from that day forward she treated me better than she treated everyone else. I guess it was part fear of Sara and part that she knew someone was watching. I guess no one really wants to be labeled as a person who bullies little children. The teacher knew that Sara would let everyone know, and it was not something she wanted said about her.

I know that the days when Sara can save me are over. As much as she wants to, it is not possible. I have to help myself, and this is the only way. Many people believe that teachers cannot be bullies, and if they see it they will stop it, but that is not true. Many of my teachers sided with the "Popular Kids" as if they wanted to be popular themselves. Some of the teachers would even join in a bit. Of course, there were ones that did not like it, but few of them did anything to stop what was going on. They either participated or ignored the taunts. I wished that Sara was my teacher because I knew that she would have made sure it never happened again.

She will also defend me to my father. She is one of the few people who will actually stand up to him. He is a hard man, and most people steer clear of him. He can con people for a period of time, but his true colors always shine through. Sara calls him on his stuff, and they do not get along at all. He knows that she knows who and what he is, and he does not like it. When she is around, he keeps the insults toward me at a minimum. This is one reason I avoid him at all costs, and I do not visit him. He makes me feel worse about myself, and that is the last thing I need. My mom and her family are all I need. We spend our lives intertwined; even our vacations are connected.

***

When our family went on our yearly beach trip this summer, it became harder to hide things from Sara. I had to get creative with my eating habits, and I had to lie a lot. I hate lying but I cannot tell the truth because it would make this process harder for me. I don't want help. I do not need help. This is who I want to be.

When we went to the beach, the trip itself was fun. Our hotel turned out to be less than expected. The hot tub was in front of our room, and because the door leading out was a sliding glass door, we could sit in our room and watch the people in the hot tub, which was awkward and funny at times. My bed was by the door. I saw people in it all night doing a variety of things. We laughed so hard about our room, and for a moment I felt normal, like I did when I was a kid. It was nice to be with my family and laugh. If only life could be this way all the time, I would not have to worry about weight and calories.

Sara tempted me with food as often as possible. A part of me wanted to eat to make her happy. This was easier when I was at home. She bought all my favorites at the store, and she ordered things that she knew I love. My family loves food and it is part of us. We love to eat, and my mom and grandma love to feed everyone. It is the Southern way, and has always been a part of our lives.

When we have a gathering, there is an abundance of food. The thought of it makes me break out in a sweat. Turkey, dressing, mashed potatoes, homemade pie and cookies have always been my weakness. How will I ever survive holidays? Maybe I will be tiny by then, and I can eat what I want, at least for the day. If Sara is able to tempt me, then how can I survive everyone offering me food? I have to be strong and not give in to temptation. It is the only way.

My Mawmaw Ruby, as we all call her, represents food and all the goodness in the world. She makes it her life goal to fatten us all up. The more we eat, the better. She does not mean any harm by it. She grew up in a different time, when people were hungry. Food was a commodity that was denied some people. She still feeds all of us as if we were starving. Most of my relatives find it comforting, but I find it terrifying. It is so hard to turn her down, and she is relentless. I will just have to continue to resist, or avoid her when possible. I know it is sad that I have to stay away from someone I love, just because I have this issue. However, it is my reality.

It is strange how we can feel as if life has changed, but in the end we are still the same inside. I will always be that chunky, middle school guy, or at least a piece of him will always be inside of me. We can change the outside all that we want, but we can never change the inside.

Sometimes I want to go back to that kid playing in the sandpile with my friends, the place where I was the boss. The huge pile of sand all the neighborhood kids played in was on my property, so I thought it made me the boss. Most of the time, while we were on my turf, they all allowed me to order them around. I would always say that

I was "king of the sandpile." The only person who ever trumped me was Sara. Even though she was an adult, she played in the sand with me and my nephew. I never made the mistake of telling her I was the boss, even though she would have probably been amused by it. She liked it when I stood up for myself, and I had many of these moments when I was young. However, then middle school came, and the pounds with it, and I became someone who invited bullying without meaning to. I became a person I wanted to hide.

    I believe we can hide that overweight person and bury him so deep he will never be found, and that is what I want to do. Bury the person I was and become someone who does not draw attention.

Chapter 2
Sara

The Chaos Starts

MY BROTHER HAS a problem, and I know it. He has lost too much weight in such a short period of time. I want him to be happy and have all that he wants in life but not at the risk of his health. Sam tells me to stay out of it, but I have never really followed his advice before, so I am not going to start when it involves my brother.

I know why he lost the weight. I would support a *healthy* weight loss plan, but I know he is starving himself. I keep thinking he will see what he is doing and just eat healthy and exercise but I know he is on a downward spiral.

I also understand being a little too chunky. I am not the queen of diet and exercise myself. I like food and it shows. The difference is that I am okay with my body the way it is, and I have never been bullied. It is like the bullies know who will take it and who will not. I have been all sizes, and I have never felt differently about myself with varying sizes. The way people have treated me has always been the same. Many of my friends obsess over a few extra pounds and dress sizes, but it truly does not bother me.

I know that Derrick has been the target for bullies for a while, and it makes me so mad I want to go to school and beat them all up. I have heard stories that my son tells me of how mean they are to Derrick on the bus and how it is worse at school. Sean does all he can to defend Derrick, but he cannot be around all the time. Sean is skinny, but tall, and his personality prevents him from being bullied. I want my brother to stand up and beat the crap out of the bullies, but that will never happen. It's not his personality. I wish he would find the fire he had when he was younger.

Once I was at the doctor's office with him when he came flying out without a stitch of clothing. I was in shock. All I could do was sit there for a minute. When it registered with me that he was escaping, I jumped up to pursue him. As I did so, my mom, the doctor and the nurses all ran out. When they caught him, they had to drag him back in. He was kicking and screaming. It took all of them to get him back into the office. He was stubborn and strong.

Later I found out that he did not want a shot, and when they told him he did not have a choice, he ran out of the room with all of them chasing him. He was so determined to get his way. I guess he let them know that there was a choice in *his* mind. Even though they won in the end, he had let them know that he had an opinion and he would be heard.

In my mind I can still see him running and all those people chasing him. He escaped out to the parking lot before he was caught and carried back in, but he sure put up a fight. I miss that fire in him. I look at him sometimes and wonder what happened to that child that could run naked through a waiting room without any care for his nudity. I want to see him feel that way again. How can I show my brother his worth when he is humiliated in every way? I know I cannot follow him to school.

There are so many theories on bullying out there. Many people say the victim should just ignore the bullies. I know this rarely works. When the target does not say anything back, they only see that as a sign of weakness and they come on even harder. Other theories tell us to report them. We all know that snitches get stitches, so that is not effective either. Personally, I think the only thing that works is to get back in their faces and fight if necessary. Winning does not matter so much as the bully knowing that the person being bullied will fight. Bullies are not accustomed to fighting because they feed on the fear of others. So when a person stands up to them, most of the time they will back down. If they do not, then I hope the person gives it his or her best shot. At least after a punch or two from the victim, perhaps the bully will think twice next time. I know that professionals will disagree with my theory. They will have much to say about how violence is not the answer, but I disagree. Sometimes it helps to get down to someone else's level. It is all the bully will truly understand.

However, all the theories in the world will not help my brother until he decides that he wants help. It has to come from him, and all I can do is encourage him to do something. I know he believes the weight loss is the answer, but I suspect it is not fixing an underlying problem, and until that is addressed, he will continue to have challenges. It cannot solve the root of the problem. I want him to be confident and happy with himself, and losing weight can make someone happy for a time, but bullies always find some new reason to torture. I know that they will start again. He has to change inside because in the end, he has to be that boy in the doctor's office who does not care what anyone thinks. That is the solution: finding that fire to fight and defend—to be confident enough with oneself to be able to run naked without any care of what other people think. How do I show him without making things worse?

Our beach trip made things very clear to me. He took long walks and swore that he ate while he was out. When I questioned him, he was very evasive. He became defensive and moody whenever I said anything about food and how he needed to eat. Mom encouraged him to eat too, but he ignored us both.

We did have some good times at the beach. Our room was horrible. It was painted burnt orange, and even though we were promised an ocean view, the only view we had was the hot tub. It only had an ocean view if we were giraffes. We actually tried to lean out far enough to see the ocean, but it was impossible. Our front door was in the parking garage and our back door was a sliding glass door that went straight into the hot tub. We gave it a variety of names, and in the end it became "the dungeon." Derrick made so many funny comments about the room he kept me rolling, and Mom was so disgruntled it made everything even funnier. When we go to the beach, she always wants an ocean view, and this room was lacking in every way. It was nice to have a reason to laugh and just be a family.

Sean kept us all laughing, and he enjoyed our room being in front of the hot tub. He made faces at the people in the hot tub, or just stared at them and giggled. When someone tried to get romantic, he had even more fun with it. I know that everyone that was trying to enjoy a blissful moment hated him, but it was not our fault they had put us so close. He was just making the best of a bad situation, and he was so funny I could not scold him.

I wished I could keep us there forever and not have to take Derrick back to endure high school. My desire to shelter him wars with my feelings that I want him to find the fight to stand up. Has he been beaten down so many times that the will to fight is gone? Will losing this weight really make the bullies stop? If weight loss works, then I believe it will only exacerbate the situation. He will see starving as the answer to his problems, and how can I argue with something that he sees as effective?

I have problems of my own with my little family. It is hard to concentrate on Derrick's issues when things are difficult with them as well. My son has epilepsy, and it is challenging to manage his seizures at times. A seizure disorder is like a constant threat hanging over the family. We always have to wonder when the next one will happen and where it will happen. There have been times that he has been injured. We had to take him to the emergency room for stitches and other bumps and bruises. We also have to time the duration of the seizures, and if they last over a few minutes, he has to go to the hospital. He is in middle school, and teenagers are complicated by design. Between work, home, cheerleading practice with my daughter and Sean's seizures, I'm very involved. I work at the elementary school with children who have behavioral disorders, and it keeps me busy.

I wish I could do more for Derrick, but I just have to hope that this is a phase and it will pass. His food obsessions are out of control, and I can see that it is getting worse. It is like watching a train wreck in slow motion. I see it happening, but I am powerless to stop it.

As we left the beach, I felt a sadness overtake me. I felt like a part of our lives came to an end. Life will never be the same again. Sean and Derrick are not children anymore and it is harder to control what they do with their lives. If Derrick chooses to starve himself, I cannot force-feed him. All I can do is offer my advice, and if it becomes more of an issue, perhaps he will go to therapy. It is the only thing I can do; I just hope it is enough.

I decided to do some research when I returned home in an attempt to help. It is the best I can do. Information is power, but I also have a feeling that he is well-informed. It is pretty obvious he knows what he's doing. He's smart and determined, and while these are generally good characteristics, I am afraid they can work against me in this instance. It will be hard to outsmart him on this one because I think he believes he has more to lose. I just have to prove to him that it is dangerous. I feel overwhelmed when I get home and when I feel I cannot take any more, I turn to the thing that helps me—kayaking.

When I am at home, the way I de-stress is to kayak. It is my way to get away from all my problems. Unfortunately, I can only go when Sam goes with me. I don't feel like I can go alone, and he will go with me on Sunday when we have a good week. Sometimes, I feel like a child being rewarded for good behavior. But I don't care. I want to go, and he provides the accompaniment that I need. If

I do all my chores, work, take care of the children and provide all of his needs, then he will take me. If I have annoyed him, or displeased him, then he refuses to go with me.

Kayaking, even with these restrictions, is so refreshing and invigorating to me. It gives me the strength and energy I need to get through the week. So what, if I have to eat a little crow so I can go. It is worth every second.

Sam and I have known each other since we were children. He was the first boy I ever kissed. I was six and he was ten. I kissed him, and informed him that I would marry him someday. He ran across the fence and ignored me for days afterward.

Sometimes, I feel as if he wants to do the same thing now. Just run away from me. He would never admit it, to me or anyone, but a part of me knows. I am too much at times, and I will never be the docile wife that worships him. I can't be something that I'm not, and he does not know how to accept the person that I am. It would be more humane to just let him go, but I am not ready yet. So, I will stay until one of us gets tired of hurting the other. I can always hope for the happily-ever-after I wanted so badly. But life has a way of teaching that happily-ever-after is really just a fairy tale for the innocent. Once that innocence has been taken, we are no longer able to believe in the fairytale. It makes me sad because a part of me died, when I stopped believing. But on the flip side, when believing stops, it can open up to a new reality. I can write my own story and be in charge of my ending. Perhaps it will be way better than a happily-ever-after. It will be different, but it could also be better.

Chapter 3
Derrick

Progression

LAST YEAR WENT well. I continued to lose weight with my starvation thing. With starving, I have to avoid the thing I love the most—food. It was not working for me, so over the summer, I found a new way—an easier way, just as effective as starving. Maybe more so. I can eat all I want. All I have to do is throw it up afterward. It is like a high. I can eat and eat and eat, and then all I have to do is puke. It is hard to hide what I am doing, but I have a whole new system. I eat when everyone goes to sleep. It's perfect and wonderful. I can be skinny and invisible. But I can eat.

If I overeat during the day, then all I have to do is take a bath and turn music on. Between the running bath water and the music, my family cannot hear me throwing up. Music is an acceptable escape for a teenager, so Mom does not think anything of it. She believes it is normal, and I get to do my new favorite thing. It is a way for me to be in control of my weight, yet I'm not doing without.

There are so many websites that can help with tips on how to do it without family knowing, and I have friends who do the same thing. There is an entire community that supports these habits. I know that most people would not understand, and that's why it's crucial for me to communicate with people who are doing the same thing. They make me feel normal and like this is not a real problem. If everyone is doing it and they are fine, then what is the big deal? I have never really felt normal, and I envy people who have spent their lifetimes being beautiful and popular. My niece, Sara's daughter, is like that.

My niece, Eva, is my role model. To me she's perfect. Eva is a cheerleader, and no one will ever make fun of her. Even though she doesn't talk a lot, everyone knows her and looks at her—not in a negative way, like everyone looked at me but in a good way. This gives me hope and relief. I could not stand the thought of anyone bullying her.

My nephew, Sean, is tall enough that everyone leaves him alone as well. His seizure disorder is not even an issue. At times, he has seizures on the bus and at school, but no one says anything to him. For this I am thankful. I never want anyone to be made fun of for anything. My nephew Sean has even defended me at times. We grew up together, and he is more like my brother than my nephew. Only a year separates us in age. We grew up playing in the sand

and riding big wheels down the bank near our home. Life felt so free then. It was so easy to just be a kid and play outside. The elementary school I went to was small, and I did not have to ride the bus that often. I wish I never had to ride the bus again. Sean loves to ride the bus. He has fun with his friends and sometimes torments the bus driver. She is an older lady and can be very grouchy. One time she was really rude to Sean, and he chewed a big wad of gum and threw it at her. It stuck in her hair. She was so angry I thought she would hit him. Instead she finished her route with the gum in her hair. The next day Sean was suspended for a month from the bus. Why didn't I think of that? A bus suspension would be a blessing to me. I loathe riding it every day.

The bus is the worst for bullying. There are so many bullies on there, and there is not a lot of supervision. The driver has to concentrate on the road, and he or she cannot look back all the time. To be honest, a lot of them do not want to know what is going on behind them because there is little they can do about the problem. They just concentrate on getting everyone home as soon as possible. This is when the bullies are able to get in their shots. It is like they know when people are vulnerable and they use it to their advantage. This year the bus has been better, but in middle school it was traumatizing. Now if I see people being bullied, I try to stand up. Sometimes, I can stop it and sometimes it just turns it on me. At least I can handle it a little better now. My weight is no longer an issue, so they have a harder time finding something to tease me about.

I guess I get my antisocial behavior from my father. Even though he can turn on the charm when he wants. I sometimes want to blame him for my issues. He was emotionally abusive to me. However, blaming him will never solve anything, and maybe I was just wired differently from the beginning. Maybe I was not meant to fit in. Now my sister, trying to be positive, would say that I was meant to stand out, but that only works if a person truly does stand out. I would be happy to fit in, or at least blend.

It is still hard to fit in. I thought that when I lost the weight, everything would fall into place. I am not sure what I expected. I guess I thought when I lost weight, I would gain popularity. Even though the ultimate goal was to be invisible, and I have achieved that, there is a part of me that wanted more. It wasn't like I expected to be prom king, but a prom date would be nice. There are girls who would probably go with me, but I will never ask because the fear of rejection is still there. It is safer to just fly below the radar. If I put myself out there, I could get hurt.

My mom and sister push me to do "teenage" things, but I just put them off. I have enough with school and throwing up to keep me occupied. Who needs football games and the prom? I have evenings filled with eating and vomiting. When I say it out loud, I feel like a loser. Every part of me wants to be normal, but I do not even know what that is anymore.

I have friends online. Most of them are socially awkward like me. They too have eating disorders. Some of my friends are anorexic, while others have bulimia like me. I understand the dynamics of both. Our mutual understanding makes it easy to be friends with them. I'm sure there are people at school who have the same problem I have, but it is harder to know for sure. It really is not a subject about which people are open and honest. The secrecy of it is part of the pact. That is one of many reasons why having friends online just makes more sense.

There are several popular girls at school whom I am pretty sure have an eating disorder. I know the signs. They either do not eat anything at lunch, or they eat more than others and then go to the bathroom. I see the ones who do not eat, staring hungrily at the plates of others, and it reminds me of the summer that I starved myself. I remember staring at food; I can still feel the saliva pooling in my mouth. Part of me wants to offer them a solution, but I am not sure it will be well received. I know that I would not want attention drawn to what I do. So, I sit there and watch, but I never say a word. A quiet observer is a part of who I have become. It makes life easier to not get involved.

Mom is concerned about the Internet access. She is worried that I will meet a predator online, but that is the least of my worries. The people I communicate with are like me. They are only interested in hurting themselves. Many of them have other activities besides eating disorders. Some of them cut themselves in places that are not visible to others, while others abuse drugs or alcohol. Eating disorders are considered an addiction; I guess it is natural that for many, it is not their only addiction. If someone has an addictive personality, then it is easier to fall into behaviors that are addictive. I did not think I had an addictive personality, but apparently I do. It bothers me to have yet another flaw, but this one I can live with because the alternative is not good. I will not be fat again, and this is the only way.

Keeping secrets from my family is impossible. My sister questions me constantly. I tease her and call her secret spy. She is not fooled by my teasing. Eventually, I know that I will have to talk to her. It is not something that I can hide forever. If I can just get a little smaller, then we can have a discussion. Maybe later I will be ready for some help. As for now, I need this to stay skinny. When high school is over, maybe it will not be as important to be skinny. Then I can seek help and ask for her advice. I know she wants to help. One day I will allow it, but not while there are bullies around. Or at least not while there are high school bullies.

What people, including my family, do not understand is when they talk about how skinny I look, it is a compliment to me. In my mind, I can never be too skinny. So, when I go to a family gathering, and everyone tells me that I need to eat, it makes my heart soar. Sara knows this is not a good tactic, but she cannot dissuade all of them. The entire time they are talking, I can see her cringing. They are feeding the fire, and they don't even know it. It makes me want to eat less, or gorge, and vomit. The control that it gives me is a high, and just thinking about it gives me a sense of happiness.

I guess I have always wanted control. When we play Monopoly, I always have to be the banker, and I always decide who has what playing piece. I made a huge deal about it when I was young. I wanted what I wanted, and I would have a tantrum if I did not get it. Once I even threw the Monopoly board just because I did not get the property I wanted. Sean knew I wanted Park Place and when he bought, it I had a meltdown. I made sure that we could not finish the game. Even though I do not have that degree of a tantrum anymore, when I play I want to be in control, and when I feel like I am losing control, I want to quit. I guess in many ways that is the way I am in life; as long as I am in control, I can deal with things, but as soon as that control is taken from me, I have a breakdown. Unfortunately, there are few things we can control in life, and I am constantly feeling anxiety. At least, I have control over my weight now. It is sometimes the only thing I have under control.

Chapter 4
Sara

Spiraling out of Control

I THINK DERRICK is throwing up, but I cannot prove it. He continues to lose weight, and it has become something that I believe is out of control. Mom says he has started eating more, but his weight is not going up—it continues to drop. I think Mom is so happy he is eating she does not see there could be a bigger problem. Throwing up is worse than starving in many ways and has many side effects. I have completed some research, and the side effects are horrific. He could lose his teeth and hair. It ruins the lining of the throat and causes many stomach problems. This is just the beginning. In some instances, it has even resulted in death. The thought makes my stomach churn.

It is difficult to prove that someone is throwing up his food. After all, we throw up in the bathroom, in private, and it is not like I can follow him into the restroom and see what he does. My attempts at listening are unsuccessful. He is good at hiding his disorder, and if it wasn't for the weight loss, I would never know. I am pretty sure he does most of his eating and throwing up at night when everyone is asleep and not hanging around.

Most people do not view an eating disorder as a serious condition. They do not think that a person can die from it, and they choose to ignore the obvious. It is viewed as a phase, and the thought is that the addict will grow out of it, or when he loses all the weight, he will just magically stop. Unfortunately, this is not the reality. The disease progresses because it is a body-image problem to begin with, and the person sees himself as fat even when he is painfully thin. When he looks in the mirror, he sees the fat person who started and never the skinny person he has become. This is a huge part of the problem. It is difficult for someone to change a perspective of himself, no matter how hard he tries.

The throwing-up part of an eating disorder, specifically bulimia, is about control. Derrick has always craved to be in control. When he was young and we all played Monopoly, he always had to be the banker. In fact, he did not allow anyone to touch the money or any of the property. If the other children touched the money, the game was over. He could not handle it without complete control. I think one of the problems with his weight is he felt it was out of control for so long. Now, like the Monopoly game, he can be in control, and he will stay there as long as it is possible. It really does not matter whom he hurts, including himself.

He is also online, and I suspect that he has found others on there with the same issue. He deletes most of his history, so checking it is useless. He teases me about being a spy, but I feel I have to do something. I know Mom is worried, but she does not know what to do either. I want him to hang out with other kids from school instead of spending the time online . . . and in the bathroom. However, we cannot force someone to make friends. Just like we cannot force someone to eat or stop throwing up. If he would admit to the problem, we could get him into a program, but the first step is admitting that it is an issue, and he refuses to admit anything. I think he knows that once he tells me, I will do everything I can to stop the problem. He is not ready for that yet.

I wish I had more time to help. I have two children who are also teenagers, a husband and a full-time job. My son's tonic-clonic seizures bring his own medical challenges, and my daughter is very active in school. Finding the time to figure out what to do is almost impossible, and proving that there is an issue is even more difficult.

The bullying has lessened, so I am sure that fact has fully justified his actions and has encouraged him to continue with whatever he is doing. In his mind it has worked, and he has to continue. How can I argue with a system that in his mind is working . . . even though in the long run it will lead to bigger problems? All that matters to him is the here and now, as is true of most teenagers.

Derrick will finish with high school soon and move on to college. Hopefully, this will take away his need to be thin, and he will start eating. If the bullies go away, then maybe the eating disorder will go with them. I can only hope because at this point I feel helpless and do not know where to turn. If he cannot admit he has a problem, then how can I make him get help? The first step to fixing a problem is to admit that there is one, and at this point no one is admitting anything.

I wish fixing this problem was as easy as helping him when he was small. Once he got his head stuck in the banisters, at my dad's house. I'm not sure why he stuck his head in them to start with but he wanted me to get him out. At first, I had to giggle. The look on his face was priceless. He was completely stuck and horrified. We tried at first to maneuver his head back through the slats, but it would not work. I think it was because his ears would go through one way but not the other. When we were trying to get his head back through, I joked with him enough to calm him down. I had him laughing a little too, even though I could see there was still a little hysteria bubbling up inside of him. Everyone was watching, and I know this only added to his anxiety. When I was sure he was not going to come out the easy way, I decided to remove one of the slats and free him. I had someone else get a hammer to get him out. I knew he would be upset if I left him. I pried the nails loose from both ends of the slat, and it came apart pretty easily. I removed the slat and he was free. The relief he felt was obvious, and it felt good to be his hero and save the day for him. However, now it is more complicated. A simple hammer will not free him from the prison that he has put himself in. There is not a tool or words to make him better now. I know my family, and I, would give anything to be able to fix the problem so easily. Everyone tries to think of a solution, and we all have good intentions. But I know what they say about good intentions: The road to hell is paved with them or something to that effect.

Our family has always been close, and we have no problem expressing ourselves. My mom's entire extended family lives on a small mountain in North Carolina. Everyone knows what everyone else did today and what everyone else did when he or she was five. It is both a blessing and a curse. We even have our church on our mountain. My grandparents started Mountain View Church in 1940, and it has continued to grow throughout the years. Living so close to the extended family is not a life for everyone, but it works for us on most days. Most people in the family applaud Derrick's weight loss without really understanding the concerns that Mom and I have. For the most part, people make a big deal about how good he looks. They go on and on about how it takes such willpower to lose weight. The concept that they do not understand is that any mention of the weight loss feeds his need to lose more. Their compliments are only making it worse. Their intentions, no matter how noble, are not helping Derrick. Even the negative comments exacerbate the situation. He looks at it all as a success for him. Even when it is not meant that way. I can tell that he loves for people to tell him that he is too skinny. I wish people would not mention it at all, but it is impossible to make it stop. There is not a clear understanding of how it works, so everyone is making a bad situation worse.

My mom and I understand the problem, and we have tried really hard not to mention anything about food around him. We do not offer food or discuss it with him; this can be very difficult because we have always made food such a part of our lives. When I was a child, we were rewarded for cleaning our plates and for eating all of our dinner. The highest praise we could ever get from my Mawmaw was when we requested seconds. Now we cannot talk about food.

Anyone who has lived with someone that has any kind of addiction understands how important it is not to feed that addiction. Simply talking about the thing that someone is addicted to can exacerbate the situation. In most cases with alcohol, drugs and even sex addictions, those topics are easily avoided. But with food it is difficult. We all have to eat. We have to purchase food, cook it or go out to eat. There is no way to completely avoid the topic, we also have to eat, whereas the other items that most people are addicted to can be avoided. An eating disorder, is extra difficult because it is something that we need. It is not your typical addiction.

Chapter 5
Derrick

The So-Called Good Years

I AM IN college and things are going well for the most part. There are still bullies here, but they are easier to avoid. They are also not as well liked, and there are people here who would stand up to them. Many of the bullies were high school jocks, and they are struggling, so they are more likely to ask me for help instead of bullying me. They are struggling because now they do not have sports to make them feel good about themselves. The college that I attend does not have a football team or that many athletics, so all they have are the academics, and the professors will not fix grades if they do not do well. There are no pep rallies and cheerleaders to make them feel important. I excel here and they fail. In many ways, this frustrates them more, but there is little they can do about it, although occasionally they will explode. They will make snide comments and try their best to make me feel bad about myself. Now they tease me for being too skinny, which is ironic. I would laugh, but it is not funny. The things they say are hurtful, but they stop quickly because they do not have their posse to laugh with them. It is not as much fun for them when they do not have an audience to attend their performance. Other students in my classes also have matured, and they do not find bullying amusing. Now my peers are more likely to stand up when people mess with me. The bullies are the least of my worries now. I have bigger issues.

My weight loss has become a problem. Everyone is aware of it now. I am aware of it now. I know at this point I am too skinny, or I am told I am. I am around 5'11 and I weigh about 100 pounds. I know logically this is too small. However, when I look in the mirror, I still see a fat person. I keep thinking that if I can just lose a few more pounds, it will be enough, but in my heart I know it will never be enough. In my mind, I will never be skinny enough. It is strange to me that I cannot *see* that I am too skinny. Why do I see the same person that was fat and out of shape? I need professional help.

***

The issue with getting me help is my gender. We have tried to find a program for me, but evidently it is harder to find a program for men. I guess men are not supposed to have a weight issue, or at least this is how I feel. I am ostracized once again. My family is frustrated and calling all over to get me help. Some of the groups said that I could attend the women's programs but they also discuss women's problems. I might feel uncomfortable. As if I don't feel uncomfortable enough, they want to add to my discomfort. There are tons of resources for women and girls but none for men. There are very few ways that I can cope, and I cannot seem to find any help.

I find drinking helps. That is what people in college do, right? Or at least that is what I tell myself, and it makes me feel better. My goal has always been to be normal or blend in, and drinking helps with this concept. When I am drinking, I can be the life of the party and everyone wants to be my friend. If I am drinking, then I do not think about throwing up. I can just focus on the alcohol and the euphoria that it brings. It is as though for a moment I have traded addictions, but the real question is which one is worse? The answer is that no one really knows. They are both bad in their own way but I need one or the other. Sometimes, I need both. Both of them give me satisfaction and escape in one form or another.

I am also funny when I drink and this encourages me to have more friends. I can make people laugh with me instead of at me. When I drink, everyone wants to be around me. For the first time, I feel invincible and everyone loves me. I crave love and acceptance, and this is a way to get it without shrinking back into my shell. I guess everyone is not happy about my new ways. My family hates it. They want me to get better. I try and get better for them. I hate to see the pain I cause in their eyes, but I feel powerless to stop my behavior.

    I tried an addiction clinic, but everyone there was a drug addict, and the facility was disgusting. When I saw roaches crawl across my food, that was enough. I knew I could not stay. The people there were also on probation and were being court-ordered to attend. They did not want to get better. They just wanted to stay out of prison. Many of them made it clear to me that as soon as they were free, they would be high. Drugs were also rampant within the facility. I was offered more drugs there than I was offered anywhere else. Sex was also freely offered and everyone was very vocal in what they wanted and needed. It did not take long to see that this place would never make me better. It would only feed my addictions and maybe even add one to the mix. I was miserable, and I knew it was not the answer to my issues.

    Whatever the solution was to my problem, I knew I would not find it here. I called Mom and she came and picked me up. I could tell she was upset. In her mind, it was the answer to my problems and now that it was not, she did not know what to do. Her frustration was very clear and it made me feel awful that I had disappointed her once again. It was a pattern I was tired of, and I knew she was tired of it as well. She wants me to be happy, but I cannot seem to find a way to be happy. It is the thing that eludes me. Sometimes I wonder if I will ever be happy again.

There are so many people that tell me just to stop. "Stop throwing up your food." "Stop drinking." "Just stop." They cannot see that I want to stop more than anything, but I cannot. It is not that easy. The first thing I did when I got home was to eat and throw up. It felt good and awful all at the same time. How can something so self-destructive bring me so much pleasure? How can I stop?

The thing people will never understand is no one wakes up one day and thinks he or she wants to be an addict. Nobody would choose the life I have, but it sneaks up one day at a time. The first time I threw up, I told myself it was just this once and I would never do it again. But the high was so good afterward that I knew I was hooked. There has to be an issue when it feels good to vomit. This is not something a "normal" person would ever do on a regular basis. The first time I became inebriated, I thought the same thing. I will drown my sorrows this one time and only do this casually. That did not work either. I liked everything about it, from the taste to the way it made me feel. For the first time I was free. People and what they thought were unimportant to me. My inhibitions were washed away by the alcohol. As soon as I started each of these things, I was addicted. Counselors would say that I have an addictive personality and I should avoid things that are bad for me. My brain knows this, but I cannot seem to stop. So now I am a drunk and I have an eating disorder. It all starts piling up. I just feel broken somehow, and I can't figure out how to put me back together. How do I stop my self-destructive behavior when they are the only things that bring me true pleasure?

The bottom line is that this is not the life I wanted, but it is the one I have. The solution is out there but the real question is, *Do I really want to be fixed?* I am afraid of the answer. Self-medicating with alcohol is working for now so that is what I will do until it is not effective. Then I will try something else.

The addiction clinic suggested that I try AA and go to meetings but I would have to go sober, and I hate social situations when I am sober. I also hate all the sharing that they do. When I hear their stories, it does not make me feel better. It only makes me want to drink. I kept the money that Mom gave me to donate at the meeting so I could buy alcohol on the way home. It was not much, but lucky for me I enjoy cheap vodka. During the entire meeting, all I could think about was the vodka waiting for me when I could sneak out. They respected my choice not to speak, but I could see the disappointment in their eyes. I am accustomed to that look. I know it well. It is frustrating to always make people look at me that way, and yet I do nothing to fix the problem.

When the meeting adjourned, I raced to the ABC store. I would have to hide the alcohol when I went into the house, but I could do it. If I am good at anything, it is hiding my habits. At least I do not drink and drive. I have to focus sometimes on the things I do right instead of all the wrong things I do. I would make myself crazy if I focus on the bad.

With the alcohol properly hidden beneath my clothing, I snuck into the house and told Mom what she wanted to hear before I went into my room for that first drink. It felt wonderful as it slid down my throat and burned my stomach. I took another drink, and I could feel the numbness sink in. Tonight I will feel better. I won't think about my challenges. My sorrows will drift away. I could get accustomed to these AA meetings because they get me the thing I want the most for now.

One evening while I was drinking a bit, I started thinking about the time Sara rescued a duck from our pond. The story is funny when I am sober, but it is hilarious when I am drunk.

When I was around ten years old, Sara hatched a duck egg in her classroom. When she released the duckling to our pond, it was a bit reluctant to leave her, and it took months before it stayed in the pond and did not try and follow Sara around. It was her duck, and we teasingly called her its mother. After it spent a year at the pond, the dam for the pond broke, and it drained the pond. When Sara came home from work, the duck was stuck in the mud in the middle of the area where the pond had been. He was obviously in trouble. Sara tried to coax him out, but it did not work. Sean, Eva, Mom and I tried as well. It became obvious that the only way to get him out was to go in after him.

The pond was now a huge mud pit. Sara had on jeans and a white shirt. She knew that the mud would be deep, so she removed her pants and got into the mud. Her shirt went past her butt and she had on underwear, so modesty was not really a problem. She immediately sank up to her knees. The further she walked into the mud, the more she sank in it, but she was determined. I could not stand for her to go in alone so I started in with her, and so did Sean. Mom and Eva stood on the dock and laughed. We were all covered in mud. Sara waded through until she finally got to the duck and got him unstuck, but he was so exhausted he could not fly. He needed to get to a water source, and the nearby lake was the best choice. Mom and Eva said they would take him to the lake, so Sara trudged over and gave him to them. They were still laughing at us, but they left to take the rescued duck. Now we were all pretty stuck in the mud. Sara got Sean out first because he was not in that far, and then she came after me. She unstuck me, and half-carried, half-dragged me out of the mud. When Sean and I got out, we all went to the water hose to get washed off before we could even go into the house for a shower. As we rounded the corner, my neighbor had just come in from work. Sara was standing there covered in mud, wearing only her shirt and underwear. Mr. Smith laughed and Sara told him there was a really good explanation. He responded, "Female mud wrestling?" She laughed and briefly explained. Before we made it to the water hose we also ran into Sara's husband, Sam, and he was not happy to see Sara in her current state. She was not fazed by his criticism; she had saved the duck and that was all that was really important. The memory makes me laugh and laugh. Mom came in and wanted to know what was so funny, but I just kept laughing. Memories are even better when I'm drunk.

Chapter 6
Sara

No More Denial

DERRICK IS GETTING worse and worse. Any denial that anyone had is gone. The days when we could ignore the obvious are over. His weight is dangerously low, and he now has medical issues. Mom has even had to get her septic tank pumped on a regular basis because vomit does not break down. It pains me to think of how much vomit it would take to fill up a septic tank to the point it has to be pumped. I know that he feels bad because of the expense and the embarrassment of the septic tank man knowing what is going on. It's not as if it is a secret. Anyone can take one look at him and see that there is a big issue. When the septic tank man comes monthly to pump the tank, Derrick hides in his room. He does not want to face the consequences of his actions.

He has agreed to go to counseling, but there are not any programs for males. I have called everywhere only to hear the same story. They either say women only or that he can come, but he will be the only male. You can tell that they really do not want him to attend because they make sure and mention that the issues will revolve more around women. The meetings themselves sound like they would make him feel worse about himself instead of better. How can that ever be helpful? It is so frustrating that he finally wants help, but there is no one who can help.

Now he has added drinking, and I know it will just escalate the problem. If he was just out drinking occasionally with a few friends, then it would be fine, but this is different. It is self-destructive. He never stops at a few. His weight is so low that I fear he will die from alcohol poisoning. It is obvious that he does not know when to stop, and most of the time the bottle has to be taken from him. He tells us that the drinking helps him forget about the throwing up, but it sounds like a dangerous trade-off to me. Which one is worse? They can both kill him.

He went to an addiction-intervention facility, but it was disgusting, and the people there did not have his problems. They were mainly drug addicts who were sent there in lieu of going to prison. They did not really want to get better; they were there to stay out of prison and maintain some of their freedom. He was offered drugs and encouraged to continue drinking by his peers. It was not the answer.

He goes to AA meetings. They are life-saving for many people, but they do not seem to help Derrick at all. I can see why they would not. If all these people were sitting around talking about drinking, that would make me want to drink. I suspect he feels the same, but I do not investigate. Mom is happy that he is doing something, so I will drop it for now. I know there are people who are helped by them, but everyone is different. Knowing Derrick's personality, I am pretty sure they are just fueling the fire. It seems similar to holding an AA meeting at the bar. The one thing the addicts want most is sitting across from them, and everyone around them is admitting that they want it too. For Derrick this is a recipe for disaster. All addictions are not the same. It is hard to clump them all together. The main culprit is the eating disorder. That is what needs to be treated. The clinic only exacerbated the problem. Now he has two issues instead of one. I feel he is drowning, and I cannot save him. If I am honest, I cannot save myself either.

My personal life is not going well. I have problems in my marriage; my eighteen-year-old son has moved into his own place. Even though Sean is old enough to move out, I still miss him. The fact that he has seizures also concerns me. However, I have to let him try. Quality of life is as important as quantity. I always say that, and now I have to practice what I preach. Letting go is hard, but Sam does not understand my sadness. He is happy that Sean wants to live on his own. Now I just have Eva at home. When she is gone, what will I do?

I feel in many ways I am just Sam's indentured servant. The only question is how long do I have to serve him to be set free? I know that I am the only one who can answer that question. I am the only one who can break the bond we made as adolescents. I have created the monster in many ways, and I have the power to break free. Just like Dorothy with her red shoes, I have always had the power, just not the motivation to use it. Leaving would take more energy than I have—with a full-time job, a demanding husband and a teenager at home. It is all too much right now.

My job as a teacher for students with behavior disorders is complex, and we have a new student, Scott, who concerns me. I was required to read his file before he came, and the administration never made me do this before. He has raped adult women, and my supervisor believes him to be dangerous. I am the only female in the room, and he stares at me all the time. It gives me the creeps, but at least I am protected at school. It doesn't help that he is huge and a bit scary-looking. Not in a thug way but a crazy way. He obsesses over everything I say or do, and he is always lurking around me. Everyone has noticed, so they have hired an assistant just to work with him. However, it has not stopped him from tracking my every move and always talking to me. I know that he would hurt me if he ever got the chance. The thought makes me nauseous. A part of me wants him to move on, but I know that wherever he goes, he will always find a victim.

At least this is a controlled environment where we can watch him closely. I hope it is enough to keep me safe. I am also worried that if we get a female student, he will hurt her. We do not allow him to visit the building next door because it has teenage girls and female teachers. We have been advised to keep him secluded, which only feeds his fascination with me. Everyone is concerned, but our hands are tied. I have to just stay alert and never let my guard down around him. The other day, one of the other teachers stepped out of the room for a second. I was sitting on the edge of a desk looking over another student's work. He pushed me down and smiled. Then, with his hand on my throat, he looked at me and said, "See how easy that was?" I kicked him and he let go. The other teacher heard the tussle and came back in and restrained him. The crazy look in his eyes will haunt me for a while. I wish I could have him expelled, but because this is a program for people with severe behavioral disorders, he cannot be removed. He is biding his time until he hurts me. It is hard to concentrate on everything when I feel my life is in danger. I just have to stay away from him and try to stop him from obsessing about me.

The weird thing is he can be so compliant when everyone is around. It is like he is purposely trying to lure me into complacency. He was exonerated from his crimes because of his low IQ, but I think he is smarter than any of us knows. It is more beneficial for him to be perceived as someone who has a mental deficit. I am sure he could easily fool anyone who administered a test to him.

He also likes to pretend he is everyone's friend, but it is a ruse. I cannot prove it, but I know it to be true. It has kept him out of prison and has landed him here, where he is free to stalk his next victim and study them in a controlled environment. He notices every little nuisance of my behavior. I feel like an animal at the zoo when he is studies me. I take some comfort in the fact that he does not know where I live, and he is secured away in a group home every night. I have to believe that staff keep close tabs on him, considering what he has done. They would not want to be responsible if he hurt someone.

There are so many changes in my world. It is difficult for me to keep up with my little family and still be there for my brother. Life has a way of consuming us, and we forget that someone we love is struggling. We want the world to stop so we can make it all better, but that never happens. I wish I had the magic formula to freeze things for a while, or at least until I can think of a viable solution. The impossibility of it does not stop me from wanting those frozen moments. Instead I will watch everything continue to get worse. We have to fix things while everything continues to spin, and at the end of the day, nothing gets fixed. Most of the time the situation only gets more out of control.

How can I fix something that I do not understand? It seems so simple, but in reality it is complicated. The issue is not the throwing up but the reason that he feels the need to do so. A person has to fix the reason, and I do not know where to begin. I think Derrick was broken long ago, and I do not know how to repair him. If I had a time machine, I could go back and do things differently. I would pick up on the signs at the beginning and be militant in my quest to stop his decline. But I cannot go back. I can only go forward.

Right now, I feel that my life is out of control. Even though I love my job, the danger is there, and I have to weigh the consequences of staying at my work. I am not sure at this point if leaving will deter Scott. I can tell that he wants me to be his next victim. I have never been good at playing the victim for anyone, so I will stay as long as possible. When Scott looks at me, I feel goosebumps. He makes my skin crawl. It is as if I can read every bad thought that he is having. The fact that he is a predator has already been established. When I read the reports, I did not know that I would be his prey. Now that I know this, it is harder to ignore his looks and his innuendos.

My husband tells me to quit, but I feel it's more about giving him control than for my safety. I know that my husband has always wanted me to stay home and be the perfect wife. Even though we need my income, he would love it if I were dependent on him. In my heart, I know that he wants a woman who will be the little housewife. It all comes down to control, and he knows that as long as I work, I will maintain my independence. Even if I stayed home, he would never own me. That fact I know for sure.

He cannot say that I do not fill the role of the housewife. I cook all his meals, do all the household chores, get his clothes ready and laid out for the next day, even bathe him and other things that are required of me. I also take care of the children, balance the household budget, make sure all the bills get paid and work a full-time job. That does not leave Sam much to do. All he has to do is work and come home. We were married young, and I think everyone believed I would be a horrible wife, so I worked hard to prove them all wrong. In reality, I overcompensated. Now it is difficult to stop doing all these things. I cannot just blame him for my servitude. It is my fault as well. He does not make me do it. I am a servant by my own free will. In many ways, this just makes it worse

I believe we have our defense mechanisms, and this behavior is part of mine. I set myself up to be needed. However, I refuse to need anything from anyone. So, even though it looks nice on the surface, it is not done for the right reasons. It is a way to make someone need me. I have to be the perfect wife and mom. I want everyone to need me, but I don't want to need anyone else. It is a form of control, and I am powerless to stop it. I suppose just like Derrick cannot stop throwing up. We all have our vices and quirks. The difference is that even though mine could hurt me emotionally, it will not kill me. The vices that Derrick has chosen can kill him. I have to find a way to keep this from happening.

Sometimes I feel I have no one to talk to about everything. I have to be the strong one. I do have one friend who lets me vent, and offers advice. We also talk about everything from politics to literature. He will debate with me and give me honest and straightforward answers. We became friends after he worked with my students in the scared-straight program. He is in prison, and when he first requested to be pen pals, I was skeptical. I talked to my husband about it, and he did not care as long as he could read the letters. I didn't care if he read them because I was not going to say anything he could not hear. It was not romantic. I just needed a friendship with someone who did not ask anything from me. So, we write weekly letters to one another. He always makes me feel as if I have a voice. With him I am just "Sara," not wife, mom, sister, daughter, teacher and all the other roles that I play. I can just be me, and that is enough. He is smart and likes to read. I would like to think I offer him as much as he does me.

His friendship keeps me sane. I met him only briefly one time. I took my students on a prison tour.

We were all lined up to talk to the inmates. This was the part in the tour when they "scared" the students. I made sure all my students were seated, and I chose the last chair available. It had rollers on the bottom, and the floor was slick. When I went to sit down, the chair just flipped over, and I went with it. Everyone struggled not to laugh, but when I stood up and took a bow, they all lost it. The inmates managed to pull it together and properly "scare" the kids, but I wanted to crawl into a hole. Luke was there that day. I remember thinking that he looked like one of the Backstreet Boys, but I was distracted by getting my charges in and out of the prison without incident. When we were leaving, the administrator in charge of the program requested that we send "thank you" cards. He gave me the addresses and I sent them out the next day. This started a friendship that I cherish. I would never visit him again, and we do not talk on the phone. I have requested that he does not send pictures, and I do not send them either. I want our relationship to be a clear friendship, nothing more, nothing less.

I feel that the times when I am more myself are when I talk to Luke and when I kayak. However, the kayaking is intertwined with Sam, and therefore can be taken away at any time. My dad will go with me on occasion, but Sunday is a bad day for him, and sometimes that is the only day I can go. Dad and I go kayaking during the week when I am able, and I cherish those times. We see more wildlife because he is quiet and we are in sync with one another. A beaver follows us sometimes, and I enjoy his presence so much. He will swim alongside of my kayak, and he does not show any signs that he is afraid of me.

My dad loves these moments because he knows how much I love the wildlife of the river. In many ways my dad and I are so much alike. We enjoy so many of the same things. My mom even says that we chew gum the same way. I love my dad, and it is pretty obvious. He was always taking me on adventures, whether it be a walk in the woods or a ride on his speed boat, I always treasured this time together. He enjoys wildlife as much as I do. Living in the country, he took me hunting once. I loved the time in the woods, looking at all the wildlife. Once when he saw a deer and raised his rifle, there was no way I could watch him shoot it. I stood up and yelled, "Run, Bambi. My daddy is going to shoot you!" It scampered off, and he did not speak to me for the rest of the trip. In my heart, I know that he did not want to kill the deer either. It is just not in him. He is a watcher of nature, not a destroyer.

A blue heron usually makes an appearance when we go kayaking, and every time Dad sees him, he says, "There is your bird." When he says it, I always smile. It makes me feel that it really *is* my bird, and it was put here for me to enjoy. Even though logically I know it is not true, for a moment, I believe. Kayaking helps me get through life and its problems.

Animals have always been important to me. When I was about ten, we had a small farm. One of the pigs was pregnant. My mom helped her deliver her babies one day after I got out of school. I was so excited about the babies, but sad when one came out tiny. Mom made mention that it would probably die because it was the runt. The thought horrified me. I could not stand by and let it die. I took it, after much pleading, and bottlefed it goats' milk. I spent all my free time feeding and nurturing the tiny creature. I named her Red because she had a red color, while the other piglets were varying shades of brown. She was special, and I knew it from the beginning.

She grew, and grew and grew. Finally, she was returned to her family, and she could hold her own. The runt had become the biggest pig of them all. She, however, did not know that she was a pig, and she followed me everywhere. When I came home from school, I would let her out of her enclosure, and she followed me all over the yard. She had the personality of a dog, and she thought I was her mom. At that time, I had three dogs, a goat, multiple cats and a pet pig. They were my shadows. They followed me everywhere.

Red became pregnant, and she ballooned to twice her size. We started calling her Big Red, but she did not mind. To a pig, the word big is a compliment. When she had her piglets, she allowed me to play with them. After all, I was their grandmother. When the time came for Big Red to be turned into bacon, I boycotted the slaying. I was not giving up until she was spared, it was bad enough that her babies had been sold. In the end, I won. No one would eat Big Red so she was allowed to spend her days with me. My mom did remind me every time I ate bacon, that it was pork. But as long as it was not Big Red, I guess I could deal with it. I know that if I had to kill my food, I would probably be a vegetarian.

Derrick loves cats. His favorite cat, the most beautiful one, lived for only a few hours. His bulldog attacked her and ate her in front of us. It was one of those horrible moments that I tried to shield him from, but I could not. We were all in the yard one day when Derrick was around twelve. He was showing us his cat, and when he put her down, the dog just attacked her. There was not any warning, and he had not shown any signs of violence toward cats before. One minute Derrick was holding her, and the next, she was being ripped to shreds. I jumped in and tried to pry her from the dog's mouth, all the while screaming for Mom to take the children inside, but it was too late. He just tore her up in front of us. I can still see the horror on Derrick's face and feel his pain. It seems that everything important to him gets taken. The unfairness of it hurts me.

I feel the same sense of helplessness now as I did then. His heartache and pain are so obvious, but I still am powerless to stop it. No matter how hard I try.

CHAPTER 7
Derrick

The Program

WE FINALLY FOUND a program at Chapel Hill, that accepts Medicaid. I had been considered sick enough to qualify for financial assistance. It is four hours away, and I will be on lock down. I know that I have to go, but I hate the idea of relinquishing control of my life to someone else and that is ultimately what I am doing. We are leaving tomorrow, and I dread it even though it is necessary. I have not decided if I can really go without throwing up my food. I have been doing it so long it feels like a part of my life, of who I am. The thought of gaining weight also upsets me.

My mom asked if I wanted to talk to my father before I left. I don't for a host of reasons. He will just be critical, as he always is, and I can't deal with the negativity right now. I want to be around positive people who will encourage me, and that word is not in his vocabulary. He is a pessimist with a mean sense of humor, and it is a bad combination. He is the last person I want to deal with. Sara and Mom are the ones I want with me.

My sister came by early to pick up Mom and me. She was her chipper self, but I could tell there was a sadness in her smile. "Are you guys ready?" Sara asked, and I gave her a smile that neither of us felt.

"Sure. I'm ready for my vacation." I said, and she looked at me with a small smile back. I knew that she loved it when I was in a positive mood.

"I think I might stay with you. I could use a vacation myself. I could read and hang out with you," she said and looked at Mom.

"Me too. A vacation would be great," Mom said, but I could see the tears pool in her eyes. Sara gave her a look that said no tears, so she quickly changed the subject.

"We can eat at Mama Dips for lunch," Sara said, and Mom nodded. Even though I have issues with food, eating at Mama Dips is something I have always wanted to do. She has a restaurant near Chapel Hill, and I have been looking forward to the food even if I cannot throw it up afterward.

"It can be my last meal," I said, trying for humor but it came out sad. And for a minute, we were all quiet and thoughtful.

"Not your last meal but your first meal as a well person," Sara said, and she smiled at me.

"Always the Queen of Wishful Thinking," I said, and she laughed. We have always called her this and she has not been offended by it.

"I am always the optimist. Annoying, right?" she said, but I shook my head no. Her positive attitude is my happy thought most of the time. In many ways we balance one another. She tries to make every situation fun while I find something wrong. My sarcasm makes her happy, and her laughter makes me happy. We match.

I decided to write goals for my time away, and I hope that I can make them a reality.

> It is my mission:
> To live a happy life in which I find joy
> in small achievements and balance in
> my labors.
> To continue to recover and find love of
> self and life.
> To be conscious of other people
> To become an individual to be trusted.
> To believe in and know key moral values
> that I promote, such as peace and
> the good news of Christ.
> To strive to obtain a balanced self-
> esteem and become closer to myself
> and Christ.

I shared my written goals with Sara and Mom on the way down. They were quiet at first, but then they told me they thought it was a great idea to set goals before I even arrived. They have so much hope for this program, and even though I am skeptical, I have hope as well. Getting better is very important to me. I want to live a normal life.

The drive went quickly, in part because Sara helped Mom drive, and she drives faster than Mom, and in part due to the fact that I was nervous about them leaving me. I was happy to prolong things by going to Mama Dips for lunch. The food was wonderful and I overindulged. It would be the last time I could do that for a while. Then I went to the bathroom and threw it all up. I knew that throwing up my food would not be an option for my time in the program, so I needed to feel the euphoria before I arrived at the hospital. Sara knew what I was doing, but she did not comment. In a way, I think she had given up on trying to stop me. She was leaving it to the professionals.

I saw Mama Dip herself on the way out. It was a treat to talk to her. She has numerous cookbooks, and her food is legendary. Mom bought a cookbook and told me that when I come home, we would cook some of the recipes. I am not sure if I want to do that or not. Eating means throwing up to me now.

Everyone who visits Chapel Hill should try her food. For a moment, I felt guilty about throwing it up. But then I remembered where I was going, and the guilt slipped away. My every move will be watched for a time, so I used this tiny bit of freedom without guilt.

Chapel Hill is a beautiful, Southern town, and I would enjoy being here if not for the reason I am here. The college campus consumes the town, and there are people my age all over the place. They looked so young and happy. In reality, although I was the same age as most of them, I felt so much older. They were enjoying their lives, while I felt as if I was wasting mine. Sara saw the sadness on my face and tried to comfort me.

"Maybe one day you can come to school here," she said and gave me her best smile.

"That would be fun, I suppose," I said without committing to the idea. All these people living their beautiful lives gave me anxiety. In my heart I could not imagine ever fitting in with them.

"You would love it here as a student," Mom chimed in.

I know they were trying to make it better, but in reality it only made me see what I will never have. I wished I could share their faith and enthusiasm, but I could not. When I did not respond, they let it go. The closer we got, the more my nerves kicked in.

***

When we arrived at the hospital, I felt my anxiety escalate until I felt as if I might have a panic attack. The hospital is huge, and I was instantly intimidated. *How can I stay in this place without my family?* I knew that if Sara was not with us, I would talk Mom into taking me home. I knew that she could be persuaded to allow me to go home. However, Sara is more determined, and she will never let me go home without at least trying this program. It isn't that she is heartless; it is the complete opposite. She wants me to get better and is convinced that this place is my only option.

I could tell Mom was nervous. She was talking a lot and fidgeting. I also knew if I begged her to let me go home, she would cry. She had to know that I was freaking out inside and that I did not want to stay. People in general freak me out, and being left me with strangers felt scary. It was difficult for her to tell me that I have to stay. I knew she did not want me to ask to go home, and she was happy to have Sara here as well.

We made our way up the elevator, and we could all feel the tension building. I wanted to cry, but it was too late for tears. I had put myself in this position; now I had to find a way to get out. When we arrived on our floor, we found it bright and cheery. There was artwork everywhere, paintings and sculptures. Art had always been my outlet, so it comforted me that the people I will be staying with like art as much as I do. It gave me hope that it would not be as miserable as I think. We signed in and then we went through the locked doors into the eating-disorder ward. I heard the locks click behind me, and the reality hit me hard. *I will be locked in here, and I will not be able to leave. My every move will be monitored. I will not even be able to go to the bathroom alone. I am very modest, and I do not like anyone looking at my body. I swim in a shirt. Because of my rapid weight loss, my skin hangs on my stomach and chest. I hate the way it looks, and the thought of someone gawking at it sends me into panic mode.* I looked at Mom and Sara and they saw the panic in my eyes.

Sara quickly started pointing out all the positives because that is what she does.

"You have a great view from up here, and they have puzzles and books . . ."

She trailed off and gave me a smile. Even though the smile did not reach her eyes, I appreciated the effort. I knew in her own way she was also telling me that I am staying. There was no room for debate. She was not someone to cross when her mind was made up. I could almost hear her say, "We can do this the hard way or the easy way." Either way the result will be the same. I will not be leaving here with them today. I was going to have to deal with whatever this program offered me.

As much as she is positive energy, I know there is another side. Her famous temper. I guess it is amplified by the fact that she spends so much time trying to save the world. Eventually, we all snap. One time that I remember was when she had a fight with her husband.

He had smacked her while they were in the car. I never found out the reason, but in my mind, there is never a reason for a man to hit a woman. And he had to be an idiot to hit Sara. When he got out of the car, she got out with him. I was in the yard. I could see her face and she was mad. She picked up a two-by-four. Her husband turned and looked at her, and at first he smiled, but then he saw the look on her face. She was going to hit him with it. There was no doubt in any of our minds. He ran to the other side of the car, and she attempted to chase him. When it was obvious that she could not catch him, she threw it at him. However, he ducked and it hit me.

"I'm sorry," she said, but before I could answer, he had her restrained on the car. I wanted to help her, but I was frozen. He was stronger than she. She fought him like a wild woman, sinking her nails into his face and neck. He let her go.

"Don't ever hit me again," she said to him, fury apparent in her voice. He looked at her, and she glared at him. It was her fearlessness showing. I knew that she would not be bullied.

Years later I told her that she was crazy for trying to fight him; she could never win. But she told me it did not matter if she won; bullies did not like to fight. Next time Sam would remember the scratches and that it would not be fun for him to fight. It was only fun when the other person allowed the abuse. She would never allow it, and now he knew.

I know that I have the ability to stand up for myself. When I was around five, my father yelled at me and my mom. He did not shut up, and at some point, I just could not listen to it any longer, so I went over and slapped him across the face. He was stunned, and so was my mom. Neither of them could believe that I would stand up to him. He was a big man, and he was loud. Most people would be afraid of him, but I was not. I just wanted him to stop yelling, and it was the only way I knew how to make him stop, even if for only a moment. He called me a brave, little son of a bitch. Looking back, it would not have been a surprise for him to have smacked me back. My mom would have tried to have prevented it, but it would have been futile if he really wanted to do it.

The story of Sara and the person I once was makes me feel bittersweet. I want to have her attitude, or the attitude I had as a child, but we are different people—

I was jolted out of my thoughts by the counselor.

The counselor came out and gave us all the rundown. My family would not be able to visit for three weeks, and then I get a visit only on the ward. It would be over a month before I could have a visit with them out of the eating-disorder ward. There was also a place where they can stay near the hospital when they come back. It was at a reduced price and was more like a home. They could cook there and everything. I could also stay there later if I participated in outpatient care. That was all for the future, and I couldn't think about that now.

Mom and Sara helped me move into my room. I had a room to myself because they didn't have another male at this time. All the girls were tiny, and they had the same haunted look I have. Mom and Sara hung around for a while, but we were just prolonging the inevitable, and they had a long drive home.

"I love you," I said because that was all I could

muster right now. I did not want a big, long goodbye, and I definitely didn't want them to start crying. It would undo me if they started.

"Love you too," Sara said and gave Mom a look to keep it short and without tears.

"Goodbye. I love you to the moon and back."

"We will see you soon, and we can write and talk on the phone."

They started for the door, and it was all I could do not to beg them to stay.

I watched them leave, and then I was alone. Really alone for the first time in my life. One of the girls came over and started talking to me. She showed me around. It eased the pain a bit. She was young. *If she can do this, so can I.*

Her name was Jackie. She was still a teenager. I could look at her and see that she had a problem. She was way too skinny. In reality, she was probably thinking the same thing about me, but neither of us could see *ourselves* as too skinny. We both thought that we are still big. It is the way for those of us suffering from an eating disorder. A part of me wants to ask her how she maneuvers around eating, and is there any way that I can still throw up my food. The thought made me feel awful because I knew that I was already setting myself up for failure. The fact that I did not ask her was a small victory for me.

Her story was different from mine. She was not

bullied, but she wanted to be a model, and models are skinny. The industry rewards women for being skinny, and she has been complimented on her tiny frame. Her parents, however, were not happy about it, and that was why she was here. She did not think she had a problem. We become fast friends because we had a lot of the same interests. I love art and so does she. We both thought that being thin is okay. It was nice to have someone who gets it and was going through the same struggles. For so long, I had not had anyone who truly understood. The other people here understood somewhat, but I felt the most connected to her. Some of the others had been here before, and they were a little preachy for my taste. I felt for the first time in a while that I had a friend.

The groups could be difficult, and it was nice to have an ally there. At least someone with whom I could roll my eyes when no one was looking. As with any counseling, they told us many things that we didn't want to hear, and it was easier to roll my eyes than to listen. Oftentimes, they pointed out the obvious, and that could be annoying.

I was allowed to write and send cards to everyone. For stress relief, I sent cards with my art work on them to my family. I wrote briefly in them about how I was feeling. I also tried to make them into a type of amends for the pain I had caused. I knew that I had brought hardship to my family, and this was me trying to say that I'm sorry, through my art. Sara sent me back funny letters and cards that she bought. She does not enjoy creating art as much as I do, but she loves to write, so her letters were long. They made me smile, and when anyone wrote me back or sends a card, I clung to each like a lifeline. This must be the way inmates feel when they receive mail from the outside world. For that moment, life was not as bleak; it was like sunshine in an envelope.

Soon, Mom and Sara were to visit. I was both excited and apprehensive. The clinicians will tell them all my dirty little secrets, and it made me nervous. I knew that I had to be totally honest, and that would be hard. This eating disorder has been my secret for so long, I don't want them to hear all of it. I am sure that they already knew most of it, but it still bothered me. To say it out loud to the therapists felt different.

**

When the day arrived three weeks later for our meeting with the family, the nurse had to give me a pill for anxiety. I knew that Sara and Mom would expect progress, but I still struggled. I was required to admit the problem in front of them. There was no going back from that. *They will know everything; I will no longer be able to smooth things over. I have to tell them all my tricks, and this will take away some of the power of the eating disorder. It has a life of its* own, and it is not willing to relinquish power yet, but I have no choice.

Sara and Mom were nervous too when they arrived. For an instant, I felt guilty because I know that they did not have the benefit of anxiety medication. We all sat down. My counselors and physicians each gave them an update. Some of the information I agreed with, and some I did not. I hated to be cubby holed as a person with an eating disorder. We are all so different, and our disease is different as well. I had learned this even more since coming here and spending hours with other people who had the same disease, but it manifested itself in many different forms.

There were the people who were obsessed with exercise, but not really food. They found ways to work out even within the confines of the program. Then there were the anorexics who refuse to eat. They thought that by moving the food around on the plate, people were fooled that they had eaten more than they had. Then there were the bulimics, like me, who ate huge amounts of food and threw it up. Many felt that we were the most slippery and dangerous. We appeared to be doing what people wanted, which was to eat, but then we cleverly got rid of it. Many people even weighed what they ate, and then put their vomit in a Ziploc bag so they could make sure they threw up as much as they ate. I learned this trick here, and even though I had not been able to practice it yet, the level of excitement that it might give me did not bode well for me being cured. That was one secret I would not be sharing. My main goal for this meeting was to make everyone think that I was well and that I could go home soon.

I managed to say all the right things, with a contrite look on my face. Some of them I meant, but most of them I didn't. I *wanted* to mean them all, but I couldn't. Mom looked so relieved, but Sara looked skeptical. She could sense "BS" when she heard it. Thank God she did not call me on it in front of everyone.

She did voice concerns, but without saying I was a liar. I was very careful about challenging her. I knew that if we got into a debate, my real feelings might come out, and I could not afford that consequence. So, I nodded and agreed with her, but I could tell that only added to her suspicion. By the end of the meeting, I had convinced most of the team that I was ready for a shortened visit in the hospital.

There is a Starbucks downstairs, and I am allowed to go with Sara and Mom. They fit me with a bracelet that will go off if I try to leave the hospital. I feel like a prisoner, but I know better than to complain. They would take away my right to visit if they thought that I wanted to leave the premises. I pictured taking a run for it, but then I thought of getting tackled by security, and this would make me only stay here longer.

Chapter 8
Sara

A Positive

WE HAVE FOUND a program for Derrick, but I can tell he does not want to go. We are trying to be as positive as possible. However, it is hard when he will be so far from home and we will have little contact with him in the beginning. I know that I would not like to be so far from home, so it is difficult for me to be a part of sending him away. It feels like admitting defeat and acknowledging that the problem is bigger than we are. I feel like a failure, and I know that Mom does as well.

The program is pretty simple. It is a lock-down unit. Much like the units in a ward for the mentally disturbed. His every movement will be monitored. He will not even be able to go to the bathroom alone, and his food intake is measured. The criteria are simple. He cannot go home until he has reached his goal weight—or the goal weight they set for him based on his height and body type. Derrick is such a private person. I know all the scrutiny will drive him crazy, but it is the only way.

They also have groups and extensive counseling. There are other people in the program going through the same thing, and I believe this will be beneficial. He has lived for a long time in a world that has not understood him. Now he will be with people he can talk to who have the same problem as he does. Even though the stories are different, they reflect the same symptoms. Mom and I will be allowed to visit, and we will be involved in family meetings and can attend certain groups. I want to be a part of his recovery, and I know that Mom does as well.

I can tell that Mom is both relieved and worried about leaving him. She has over-focused about him for so long it has to be a relief to leave him where he will be taken care of. She needs a break, but it is also hard for her to give the control to someone else. Mom is a natural at nurturing. I am sure that my independent spirit drove her insane. She always says that I came out of the womb wanting to do things for myself. If I am honest, I am dreading the fact that she will not have him to focus on. The attention will stifle me.

***

The drive home is quiet. Mom and I are both lost in our thoughts. There are so many things going through my mind about Derrick and life in general. I suggest we stop at a nice place for dinner, and she readily agrees. We can eat without worrying about Derrick and what he is thinking about the food or if he is going to throw up. I know it is the first time in a while that Mom can eat without care. She eats more than she has in a long time, and it makes me happy to see her enjoy her food. For a time, food does not have to be an issue in our family. We can eat without guilt. The weird thing is I normally feel good about seeing the positive, but in this situation I feel bad. I mean I am happy that we do not have to deal with the food issues of my brother and we can focus on other things, but this makes me feel as though I am betraying him in some way.

    Guilt is one of the many emotions I feel when it comes to Derrick. When I have a sibling who is not well, I feel it is somehow my fault. It makes me feel guilty for being healthy. Because I also have an older sibling that passed when I was young, I have to add survivor's guilt into my current equation. I know that Derrick's illness is not my fault, and I do all that I can to make it better, but somehow I still feel responsible and guilty. I know that Mom also feels guilty, and I try to tell her all the time that this is not her fault. However, I can tell that doesn't change the way she believes. As women, I think we always have to believe that we did something wrong when it comes to people who depend on us, and that make us have these feelings of guilt. An eating disorder is a disease. If I need to blame anyone, I will blame the bullies for torturing him when he was young. I'm not sure if they would feel guilty, but that is where I would place blame. Sometimes it is too much, and I need a reprieve.

***

I want to go kayaking to get my mind off Derrick, but Sam refuses to go with me. He has always used kayaking as a reward and punishment system for me. When he refuses, despite knowing what I am going through, it is a light-bulb moment for me. How can he be so cold to someone who has done so much for him? I ask so little, and that he would deny me this when I'm experiencing a very tough time is empowering for me. Knowledge is power. I do not need him.

I can go alone. I know what I am doing. I never tip over. He is the one who turned over last time and I had to help him. I can do this, and with this thought, I go. I load my kayak and go alone.

It is so peaceful. It is actually much easier to go alone because I do not have to limit how far I go or the speed that I travel. I am faster than most people, and I normally spend a huge portion of my time when I am with others, waiting on people. I am not limited this day. This is so representative of my life. It is limitless, and for so long I had thought it was limited. I see now that I have the key to happiness, and it has been a huge mistake to place the key to my happiness in Sam's hands. I do not need him to do this with me. It is a thrill that I did not know I could have. If I don't need him for this, could I be without him all together? Would being alone really be so bad?

I think people believe that being alone is the worst thing that can happen, but I disagree. It is much worse to feel alone when with someone. The difficult thing is finding wings to fly away. A part of me wants to believe in the fairy tale. Leaving Sam will end believing in happily ever after. However, one day I believe I will be ready to leave; this is a step in that direction. He is teaching me that I do not need him at all; I am not sure he understands what that means. But he will. It will be too late, but he will understand.

Chapter 9
Derrick

Home Sweet Home

I AM HOME from Chapel Hill, and I have continued to cope even while drinking and binging. Nothing has really changed. Now I have the information I need to quit but just not the desire. They can give me all the skills in the world, but if I refuse to use them, they are useless.

Drinking helps take my mind off everything. It is my go-to answer. If I am upset, drink. If I am hungry, drink. It is good for whatever ails me. It is also really easy to throw up alcohol.

I am at the weight that they (whoever they are) feel I should be. I feel fat and I cannot wait to get some of the weight off. I have to bide my time because everyone is watching me, and I do not want to be sent back. Drinking helps me, but to get money, I have to hoard every extra penny until I can save enough for a bottle. Then I have to tell Mom a thousand lies to get it. Then I have to sneak to the store. Then I have to sneak it in the house and drink it. When the vodka hits, I don't care about anything, so it takes away the lies. It is hard to hide the fact that I am drunk from my mom. She worries about me, so she hovers.

Sometimes I can beg Mom, and she will buy some for me. I can tell that it bothers her and makes her feel like an enabler, so I only ask when I am desperate. I would rather leave her out of the equation. It is enough that I feel awful. Why bring her into my black hole? I know that I suck her into my abyss way too much. The thought hurts me because I love her so much. There is a part of me that wants to leave so she can have a normal life and not have to spend all of it worrying about me.

I think about Sean living on his own, and I think that could be me. I have my driver's license and an education. However, this disease cripples me, and I cannot do anything without obsessing over food. I am also so skinny now no one would hire me—or people tell me I am skinny; to me I am still fat. I have very low energy, and it is hard to function. Sean has seizures and cannot drive, but he works. It makes me feel worse about myself. My family does not bring it up, but they don't have to because I know. The thought of it all makes me sink more deeply into the hole I have dug for myself. I want a drink even more now. I just want to sink into oblivion.

The one thing that still brings me joy is my art. I love to create. It is my passion. My one downfall is I want it to be perfect, so I end up throwing away many pieces, before I keep one. While I was in the hospital, I started creating cards and notes for people. It was my way of giving back for everything my family had done for me. I want to give them the joy I deny myself. I have continued this since I came home, and it gives me something to focus on for a moment. The flip side is it also stresses me out if they do not come out as I want them to. I realize it is crazy to have the thing that makes me feel confident also be the thing that stresses me out.

Sara took me kayaking to help me de-stress. I was a bit nervous, but she knows what she is doing, and I trust her. There are so few people whom I trust. I don't really know where I lost my trust in people. I think that the bullying did not help, and there were so not many who came to my defense when I was in school. It made me cynical and non-trusting about the world in general. Now I have a very small circle, and I cherish the few individuals that I allow in. The trip was actually peaceful, and I felt good that I did not flip over. I am surprisingly comfortable in the kayak. I balanced well, and did not feel like I was going to fall into the water. We saw a great, blue heron and a variety of other birds. Sometimes, I know Sara sees otters and beavers, but we talked a lot today, and we were not lucky enough to see them. Sara told me that I did great, and she wants me to go more often. It was peaceful, and for a moment I did not think about throwing up or drinking.

Sara goes kayaking all over the place, and I know that it is her release. She craves kayaking like I do alcohol. It is her drug. I wish that my addiction could have been something positive, but I have learned that this is not in the cards for me. I will enjoy this day with my sister, and later, I will deal with my demons.

There are so many moments with my family that I want to enjoy but I cannot. Thanksgiving is one of the holidays that is very hard for me, and for that matter anyone with an eating disorder. It is a holiday that is food-based. And it is buffet-style, which makes things even more difficult. My family members are superb cooks, and the food that is laid out is spectacular. There are so many things that are my favorite, and resisting can be hard.

Then I cannot really binge in front of everyone. They would be happy, at first, but when I go to the bathroom afterward, they will know why. So I am forced to eat, but not as much as I want, and not as much as everyone would want. It makes me feel like a disappointment. I cannot even handle Thanksgiving without drama.

Mom makes all her special dishes, and I know that all she wants me to do is enjoy, and I wish I could. I think people think I want to be this way, but I would give anything to be normal. To be able to go to a dinner without severe anxiety. Everyone knows that I have been in and out of the hospital, so I know they are watching me, wanting to see if I eat.

Then if I make a small plate, I can hear the whispers. I know some of it is paranoia, but I feel their eyes on me. I also know that they are truly concerned, so I try not to get agitated. They are worried about me. I eat as quickly as possible, so I can go home. I know Mom wants me to stay, but I have to get away. After our Thanksgiving meal, I stay for as long as I can stand it, then I make an excuse to leave. I have to get home to throw up. Even though I didn't eat that much, I need to get rid of it.

Mom looks disappointed when I leave. She knows what I am going to do. However, she lets me go and she stays. I know that I have dampened the mood for her. She will stay but worry about me. I want to reassure her that I am fine, but the words will not come. I get tired of the lies. They have become a part of my life, but I do not enjoy them anymore. At first, it was fun to fool everyone, and make them wonder. Now they know, and the secret is out. They know all my self- destructive behaviors.

When I get home, I immediately go to the bathroom and throw up until there is nothing left in my stomach. I do not have to stick my finger down my throat any more. It happens with little effort now. All I have to do is envision the mounds of food, and it comes out. After I throw up, I take a bath. I need to relax and let my anxiety seep out. I heard Mom come in half way through my bath. She sees that I am in the bathroom, and I can feel her pain even though she is not in the room with me.

Chapter 10
Sara

Healed (Not)

DERRICK IS BACK home, but I can tell that he is not well. He still has the same obsessions about food, and he has continued drinking. Mom is trying to be positive, but I can tell she is worried. We put all this hope into this program, and it did not work. He has gained weight, but he is not well. I try not to show my disappointment to Derrick. He is struggling, and I know that he wants to be well. The drinking is very prevalent right now. I don't know how he is getting the alcohol, but he seems to find a way. Mom does not like to buy it for him, but I know that she sometimes gives in. She does not have the willpower to deny him. This benefited me when I was young, so I cannot fault him for using it. Mom never wants us to hurt, and she has never been a disciplinarian. It is easy to get her to do what you want.

I know that we have to do something. I lost my older brother when I was ten, and the thought of losing another one terrifies me. It is not something I ever want to go through again. My older brother was seventeen when he was murdered in our home. My mom and I came home after she had finished her job on second shift. When we arrived home, she was surprised that my brother's car was there. He was supposed to be gone for the night. I went and crawled into bed, while my mom went to talk to him. His door was locked, and I heard her call for him. Then she went to the kitchen to get a knife to open his door. I heard her trying to get it open, and she called for him, confused this time. Then I heard screams, the kind of scream that pierces the soul, the kind never forgotten.

I jolted out of bed to see what was wrong. I followed mom into the kitchen, where she was hysterically calling my grandparents. She grabbed me and held me sobbing and murmuring NO over and over. When my grandparents arrived they called 911, and my grandmother went to see my brother. My grandfather told me to get a wet washcloth for my mom. The bathroom was beside my brother's bedroom. I saw my grandmother inside and she was wailing and holding my brother in her lap. I went inside, and it was then that I saw him. He had a hole in his head, and there was blood and other stuff everywhere. My grandmother was washing his face, but even I knew that it was too late. I backed out of the room and walked into the kitchen. By then the emergency medical people had arrived, and my extended family. They whisked me away to my grandmother's house. I could not fully comprehend what had happened.

For the next few days, my mom would get hysterical if I left her sight. I wore my nightgown until someone in my family brought me clothing. Mom refused to go back to the house, so they just got me new stuff. I felt hysterical inside and confused, but I had to be strong for my mom. My dad finally saw that I needed a break, and he took me for a walk and described death to me. It was a lesson I did not want. It was a conversation I know he never wanted to have with me.

After our walk he took me to buy clothing for the visitation and the funeral. I refused to wear black; instead I insisted on buying white. My brother would hate black; he would hate the depression of it all. He would want me to wear white. My dad allowed it, and I'm not sure Mom even noticed. The visitation was horrible. All those people gawking at my brother in the casket. Most of them did not look sad. I wanted to punch them. If they could not be sad, then I wanted them to leave. I would have yelled at them all, but I knew that it would only upset my mom, and the last thing I wanted to do was cause her additional stress. After the visitation, my dad and stepmom took me to dinner. I needed the break from all the people, I felt like I wanted to snap, scream and have a full blown temper tantrum. But instead I held it together. There were so many whispers about what happened, and I was tired of hearing it all.

The funeral was equally bad. My mom threw herself on the casket, and family members had to pull her off. I felt helpless. There was nothing I could do. A part of me, the part that did not understand death, wished I was the one who was dead. I felt my mom would have been less upset if it would have been me. I just wanted her to smile again, and be happy. I would have done anything to have her just be happy. After the funeral, we tried to get back to normal, but it was so hard. Three weeks after my brother's death, Mom was apologizing to me about my brother dying. She said she was sorry and did not want me to worry about my brother. I told her I was not worried about my brother, that he would be fine. I was worried about her. It was as though a light bulb went off for her, and she started to live again. Day by day, she healed a little. I knew that she would never completely heal, but now she lived, and I knew it was for me. How can she go through that again? How can I? Life cannot be that unfair.

***

I have started a new job as a probation officer. The other day, Scott showed up at the courthouse while I was working.

"Hello, beautiful," he said, and it made chills go down my spine. I wanted to run away, but I refused to let him scare me.

"Scott. What are you doing here?" I asked, trying to keep the fear out of my voice.

"Visiting a friend," he said, looking me up and down suggestively.

"Who is your friend?" I asked, again trying to make him see that I knew he was a liar.

"That's private," he said and smiled.

"I have to get back to work," I said.

"I need to show you something outside. It's important," he said and pointed to the door.

"I need to get back to work," I said. He looked like he wanted to pull me out, but there were people around. I felt that if there were not people around, I would be in trouble.

"Until next time . . ." he said, and I scurried away. When I looked back, he was staring at me with a scary look on his face.

The fact that he acted nonchalant about the entire incident bothered me—his boldness and lie when I knew he was there for me. He tried to get me to go outside with him, but I knew better. In what universe did he think I would leave with him? He wants to hurt me. I ignored him and went into a part of the building where he could not find me. For the rest of the day, I could not get the image of him out of my mind, his staring at me as I walked away and his eerie promise of seeing me later. I do not want to see him later.

 I notified his case manager that I saw him. It was close to the end of the day, but he still took the call. He knows how dangerous he is, but he also has to be his advocate. He was sympathetic, but I did not have any real proof that he was there for me. I am sure that I sounded narcissistic, but I do not care. I have to tell someone. I want them to know that he is stalking me. At least, there is a record that I called, and I had concerns.

 Later on in the day, his counselor called me and told me if I saw him again to call the police. The case manager had notified her, and I could hear the concern in her voice. It both relieved me, and terrified me, that she knew he was stalking me. I could tell that she wanted to say more. She could not give me specifics but was concerned for my safety. Scott had told her his plans for me. I wanted to know more. I wanted her to go to the police with me. But I know that she has done more than she was supposed to, just warning me. The thought of what he wants from me makes me nauseous.

 I left the school to get away from him, but he has found me. How will I ever get away from him completely? It's like he has nothing better to do. The thought of a rapist setting his sights on me is disturbing enough, but he could hurt me. He wants to, I can see it in his eyes. He doesn't just want to have sex with me. He is one of those people who feel, If I cannot have you, no one will. When he figures out that I will never willingly be with him, he will hurt me. The thought makes sick to my stomach. I have too much to do to worry over it. I have to move on, and just take precautions. Life has a way of making a person tough. I have other issues to focus on now.

***

Sean is doing well on his own. I am so proud of him. He had every excuse to stay home and receive disability because of his seizure disorder, but he made the choice to work, even though it is not as easy for him to find, and keep, a job. Sometimes when I leave him living on his own, it is hard for me. The "What ifs" hit me. What if he has a seizure and he lies there all night? What if he does not take his medication? What if he hits his head when he has a seizure? What if he doesn't eat properly? All the worries that a mom has are multiplied because of his seizures. However, I have always said that quality of life is as important as quantity and sometimes I have to practice what I preach. I will pray for him and put my worries in God's hands.

Sean has tonic-clonic seizures, and they can be very scary. Oftentimes, when people witness one, they do not want to be alone with him again. This makes employment a problem. He has managed to maintain a job, and they brag on how hard he works. He is a dishwasher at a local pizza place. He comes home smelling of pizza and spaghetti. However, he likes the people he works with and does a good job.

When he was young, I made him wash dishes if he made bad grades. I would reiterate to him that if he did not do well in school, he would have to work hard. Every time someone brags on his work ethic, I always smile, and he laughs. I tell him I prepared him. Ironically, his first job out of high school was washing dishes. It was a skill set I assisted him with in his youth. He has done well, and I want the same for Derrick. However, he continues to have problems.

Mom and I had to take Derrick to the hospital. He passed out, and we knew it was from dehydration and malnutrition. When we got him there he had been drinking a little before, and the hospital staff had little patience with him. I think they believed he just passed out drunk, and they were not seeing the bigger picture. I wanted them to do something for him. Maybe they would have the miracle that we need. They have to try. I felt desperate and crazy. I wanted him to be well. I wanted them to help me and Derrick.

The longer we were there, the more I knew that they had no interest in helping him. At best, they might put him in the mental ward for a few days. Their nonchalance was infuriating; couldn't they see how sick he was? I tried to talk to them.

"It isn't the alcohol," I said. "He's not drunk. He is sick."

"There is little we can do for him. We will give him fluids, but the rest is up to him," the physician told me.

Derrick was listening and I could see that he was getting angry. I was angry as well, so I did not try and calm him down.

"There is nothing you can do?" I questioned the doctor, fury bubbling up inside me.

"No," he said. The blank look on his face sent me over the edge.

"You are just going to let him die? Isn't it your job to save people?" I said, and I felt hysterical. Mom was quiet, and she looked more sad than angry. I wanted to calm down, but it was impossible.

"I can only save people if they want to be saved," the physician said. Derrick was hearing our conversation, and at this point, he had experienced enough as well. He had an IV in his arm, and he ripped it out. Blood spurted everywhere. The nurses rushed to contain him, but they were told by the physician to let him go. They handed me some bandages. I helped Derrick gather his stuff. He was out of control, but I was too.

I looked at the physician on our way out.

"He's going to die, and you did nothing to save him," I said, and his eyes met mine. There was a sadness in his eyes that only further infuriated me. "His blood is on your hands." I walked out of the hospital with Derrick in tow. Mom followed us, looking as if she was going to cry. I am sure we looked crazy with Derrick bleeding, half in his clothes, and cursing the hospital.

I feel helpless. The more I try to help, the worse it seems to get. I can't let the doctor be right. *I will save Derrick, even if he does not want to save himself.*

Chapter 11
Derrick

Saturated

My drinking has taken over my life, but I cannot admit that to anyone. As a matter of fact, everyone is pissing me off. I am an adult. I can do as I please. I know that I still live with my mom but shouldn't. I have a right to some privacy. My family keeps trying to do an intervention. They just have an issue deciding what is worse—the drinking or the eating disorder. Tonight I got really drunk, and I felt like killing myself. I fell in my room and Mom found me. There are many things that I do not remember. I remember pain in my shoulder, trying to fight my sister and waking up in a hospital with a police officer standing over me. The officer did not look happy, and my sister looked pissed and upset. I was too out of it to care, and all I really wanted to do was fight with them both.

"What are you staring at?" I had angrily snapped at Sara.

"A spoiled brat who needs to grow up," she quipped. And the officer smiled, which further annoyed me.

"I'm getting out of this bed and leaving," I said, attempting to stand. The officer stood up as well.

"If you try to leave, I will have to use the Taser on you," he said and looked at my sister.

"Go ahead. Hand it to me. I will do it myself," Sara said, and I could tell she meant every word. I had gone too far with her. She had finally snapped. I know she is normally patient, but I had pushed her to her limit.

"Where's Mom?" I asked. Mom would be nice to me no matter how far I had pushed her.

"She's in the waiting room, and she is not coming back. Tonight you are stuck with me, and when I leave, you have this nice officer to supervise you."

I felt helpless and frustrated. Mom would never leave me here without her being close by. It was worse than I thought. A nurse came in. "Make Sara leave," I told her.

"She can go, but the officer stays," the nurse said.

I could tell I had exasperated *her* as well. I wish I could remember everything I had done over the course of the evening. "Am I injured?" I asked.

The nurse sighed. "Yes. Your shoulder is broken, and you will be on suicide watch for a while." Sara was gathering her stuff, and I could tell she wanted to leave. A part of me wanted to beg her to stay. I wanted to apologize for everything, but my pride would not let me.

"Goodbye," Sara said. "I truly hope that you get the help you need. If not for you, then for Mom. You are killing her." She turned to leave. I let her walk out, and I had a brief panic attack that I might not ever see her again. In my heart, I knew she would forgive me, but the thought of her walking away forever terrified me. I had so few people in my life who truly loved me, and I knew that she did. I let her go. The officer shook his head. I knew what he thought of me, and it hurt. The nurse came in and gave me medication, and for the first time, I took what was offered. I wanted to sleep and forget this night happened.

The next day, I realized what I had done. Even though I was still angry at Sara, I was more embarrassed. I was expected to be at the hospital for a few days until I could convince everyone that I would not kill myself. When released, I planned to contact my father, even though I loathed the idea.

I called my father to pick me up at the hospital, thinking that maybe I might stay with him for a while, but after a brief conversation with him, I knew I could not. I wanted to go home, and he agreed to take me to my mom's house. I knew Mom would be there for me, as she always had been. I knew she was not happy with me, but unlike my father, she wanted me home. The good news was it did not bother me that he did not want me. I was past the point of caring about his opinion of me.

When I reached home, my Aunt Judy was there. It was good to see someone who had not been there while I *showed* myself. It took my mind off things to talk to her for a moment. We had always been close, I think in part because she liked to paint and do art work. She did not have children. All her nieces and nephews were like her children. Her husband was a quiet man, and I felt he was a father figure to me. If I could have chosen someone as a father, he would have been a good choice. It eased my anxiety to have Aunt Judy close today. I knew that she was aware of what happened; that is the thing about a close family—everyone knows everything about everyone. That is the bad news, but the good news is that they know all the bad and love anyway.

I hoped Sara could forgive me and make things easier. It would hurt me to think I had lost her love. In reality I know that will never happen, but I have pushed her pretty far this time.

I know that she always has my back. Even when I was small, she tended to me when I was really hurt. Mom became hysterical if she thought I was seriously injured. Sara was so accustomed to Sean's seizures she was the person I wanted around in a crisis.

After I had my big wheel accident when I was small, Mom was completely out of control. I knew it was bad because there was blood everywhere, but Sara remained calm while they took me to the hospital. My wounds had to be cleaned, and it took numerous people to hold me down. I was a spirited child. I want that person back so badly. I wish I could go back to the first bully, and when he insulted me, I would punch him in the face. I think it would have made all the difference. But I can't go back to those days or the ones where Sara could kiss my boo boo and it would be all right. Now all she can do is watch me spiral. I know this is the real reason behind her anger. She is also upset because Mom stays stressed out. I know she is right, but it isn't like I want to be this way. I want to be better. I want to be "normal." I just don't know how.

Mom has been quiet about the entire incident. I know she is really on Sara's side. After all, *I* was the one acting crazy, and Mom did call Sara. But Mom is the type of person who will not mention again the time I spent in the hospital. She will just try and move on from it and hope everyone forgets. Sara will not make things as easy, but I also know she will forgive me.

When I finally see Sara, she is more quiet than anything. I know I have hurt her when she is quiet. Again, I want to tell her I am sorry and will never do it again, but "actions speak louder than words." So I will *show* her. I need to change, and this gives me the incentive I need.

Chapter 12
Sara

Words Can Hurt

DERRICK TRIED TO kill himself, and Mom called me to come and help her. She had to be desperate to ask for my help. When I arrived, he was passed out on the floor. He appeared to be injured, but it was hard to tell how badly. We drove him to the hospital after I had to practically carry him to the car. He was so drunk I was afraid that he had alcohol poisoning. At least he was cooperative when we were getting him to the car. When he came to, all he wanted to do was fight. I had to restrain him all the way there because he tried to jump out of the car. I could tell Mom was terrified that he would succeed and the results would be really bad. I held him in with his arms crossed over his chest so he could not get free. When we arrived, I had to fireman-carry him in and then restrain him in a wheelchair. The nurse at the waiting room called an officer when she saw that he was fighting me. "He is suicidal," I informed her. I managed to check him in and hold him at the same time. I wheeled him into the waiting room while he cursed me continuously. Mom sat quietly near us.

"My sister is a whore," Derrick said loudly to the entire waiting room. They were already staring, and now they were riveted on our little drama.

"My brother is a drunk," I said.

Everyone shook their heads.

"I'd rather be a drunk than a whore," he said.

I sighed. I wanted to throat punch him. "At least the only person I hurt is myself," I said. In my heart, I knew it was the alcohol calling me a whore. However, I was tired and scared, and I had enough of his drama. Before we could argue anymore, a nurse called us back. He wanted Mom to come with him, but I told him he was stuck with me.

He started to protest, but I rolled him back in the wheelchair. When we got to the room, he told the nurse that he wanted me to leave. She had observed the drama in the waiting room, and she knew that I was better equipped than she to handle him, at least until the police arrived. After a quick look, the doctor decided that his shoulder needed to be x-rayed. I had a blissful few minutes when they took him down. By the time they got back, he had an attitude and was arguing with everyone. They were happy to leave him with me. The officer came in at the height of Derrick's temper tantrum, and when my brother tried to escape, the officer grabbed his wrist and twisted it backward. Derrick got back in the bed. *I need to memorize that technique,* I thought.

We sat in silence while Derrick gathered his energy. Then he would either curse me out or try to escape. He always started his tirade by saying he wanted me to leave. Finally, after the officer threatened to tase him, I took him up on his offer and left. I knew they would put him in the crazy ward for a few days where he would at least be safe. For now, it was the best I could hope for. A part of me hated to leave him, but a bigger part of me couldn't take any more today.

There comes a time when I have done all I can do, and I have to let it go. I am at that point with Derrick and other things in my life. I can't save everyone. Maybe it is time I concentrated on saving myself. I want to go home and be with my family.

My husband and I are still having issues, and I feel I need to be there to fight for our marriage. He did not care enough tonight to even offer to help me with Derrick. I try so hard not to be bitter, but at times like this, it is difficult. We have known each other since we were children, but there are days lately I feel I don't know him at all. He no longer seems like the man that I married. If I am being honest, I am not the same person either. But at least I want our marriage to work and he does not. It feels as if he has given up, and I am powerless to stop this descent. I feel I can't save Derrick, and I can't save my husband. I guess with both of them, I will give it my best shot, and if I fail, at least I know I tried my hardest.

There are times I believe that if I would have been an obedient, stay-at-home mom, Sam would love me more. He is the type of man who needs his wife to need him, to believe that she cannot survive without him. He knows that will never be me. I will always be able to stand alone. I will never need him, and that is some of the problem. I will not take all the blame, but at least I try to understand life from his point of view.

***

I had a dream in which Satan was trying to take me and my family. It was the most vivid dream I ever had. I was really battling him. We were in my home, and everyone else was asleep. All the windows in the house were open, and wind-borne debris was flying in from outside. I stood in the middle of the house, ready for battle.

"You can't have us," I screamed.

I heard laughter—scary, diabolical laughter. I felt a deep fear. How could I fight Satan? It was impossible. Then a peace came over me. I could not, but Jesus could. I smiled and started singing "Jesus Loves Me" at the top of my lungs. The singing that came from me was not pretty, but it was loud and full of confidence. The more I sang, the less the wind blew, and the fear started to slip away. Slowly the wind died completely, and then the windows slammed. I stopped singing. I felt safe. Then I heard the whisper of these words,

"You saved yourself and your children, but you will never save him." I felt the coldness of these words, and I jolted awake. I looked over at Sam sleeping, and I felt deep sorrow. I wanted to wake him up and beg him to save himself. But I knew he would not listen. I could not save him. It broke my heart. Many would tell me it was just a dream, but I knew it was more.

The days that followed had put me in a funk. It is hard to watch someone I love kill himself slowly, like my brother was doing, and to watch my marriage dissolve. It is too much, and my sister saw it. She could always sense when I was at my limit. Usually, a drive and dinner would recharge me. However, this time I needed more. I craved an adventure and a chance to get away.

My sister convinced me to take a brief reprieve and go to Canada with her. She called me one day while I was at work.

"Let's go kayak with whales," she said in her double-dare tone.

"When?" I asked and laughed a little. I was in the middle of work, and the idea brought happiness to a mundane day at the office.

"Next week?"

I laughed, but there was a serious tone in her voice.

"We have to stop talking about it and just do it." She paused, then pressed on. "We are not promised tomorrow," she said, "and I want to do it. While we can,"

"How about money?" I asked, trying to figure it all out in my head.

"I have copper wire to strip that we can sell for money. And I know you have more vacation hours and comp time than you will ever use. Let's just go," she pleaded.

"Okay. Let's go," I said, and she screamed and I knew she was dancing around her living room.

"We are going to kayak with whales," she said, and we both laughed.

Getting the time off was a little more complicated, but in the end, my supervisor allowed me to go. I felt an urgency I could not explain. It was as if it was now or never.

We have always wanted to kayak with whales in Canada. We would worry about the consequences later. Sam stays mad at me anyway . . . might as well give him a reason to be mad. When I told him, he did not really react. I believe he was happy to be rid of me for ten days. I would not think about it; if I did, it would put a damper on my excitement.

We left for ten days of sightseeing and kayaking. We kayaked alongside humpback whales, belugas and other whales. We had lobster in Maine and visited Niagara Falls and a butterfly farm. It was the trip of a lifetime, and I have no regrets about going.

Luckily, my new job allowed for such trips. If I had been working for the school system or as a probation officer, then I would not have been allowed to leave on such short notice.

***

I work as a case manager for individuals with disabilities, and I love the switch from youth with behavior issues. I enjoyed my previous job, but it was time to move on to something different. It is interesting that I chose this career path because in college, I could not imagine working with people with severe disabilities. I thought I would feel badly for them, but the opposite is true. They do what they want, when they want (for the most part), and they really do not care what people think. There is a freedom in their attitude that I will never have, and I am envious.

I have one client who will strip naked and do gymnastics when she feels like it. She does not care that she is a little chunky and that nudity is frowned upon in society. It is what she wants to do, and damn the consequences. She will do it in true Olympian style, while her respite workers chase her and try to redress her. All I can do is giggle because really, who doesn't want to do gymnastics naked at Walmart?

My clients with disabilities teach me so much about love and acceptance. When I go to the workshop to visit, they tell me I am beautiful, no matter how my outward appearance looks. They are looking at the inside. They could care less if my clothes match, or if my make-up is perfect. All they care about is whether I am kind to them. If only everyone were the same. Their measurements of wealth and love are so different and so much more God-like than anyone I know.

At the end of the day, I feel sorry for the "normal" people. They will never know the freedom and purity that my clients have.

You are
my

Chapter 13
Derrick

Repeat

I AM GOING to Chapel Hill again. I guess the hospital thing has made me see that I need help. I hate to argue with Sara, and the fact that I called her a whore at the hospital haunts me. She has forgiven me but I can't forgive myself. I try not to think about that night in the hospital. I was angry for a while, but I know what happened was my fault. The first step in recovery is admitting that I have a problem. I have a big problem.

My mom and grandma are driving me down. Sara usually goes, but she has a lot on her plate now. She is getting a divorce and her half-sister is sick. Christina was diagnosed with Stage IV breast cancer. I don't know how she deals with everything. I know in my heart that I add to her stress but she rarely complains.

This trip to Chapel Hill will be exacerbated by the fact that I will also need to detox from the drinking when I arrive. They will have to deal with that problem before we can even start working on the eating disorder issues. Mom seems happy that I am going, and I know that a part of her is relieved that I will be someone else's problem for a few months. She would never admit it out loud, but I know it's true.

When I arrive, there is some of my art work on the walls and there are also familiar faces. This fact makes me feel better even though it should not. I should want them all to be healed, but the fact that they are not makes me feel less like a failure. This disease is hard for everyone who suffers, and seeing them gives me comfort. I suppose the phrase, "Misery loves company," applies to this situation. The first time I came I was a lot more nervous because I did not know anyone. At least now I have friends here who understand me. I also know how to work the system here, to gain the maximum amount of weight in the shortest time. I know I should concentrate more on getting well, and less on going home, but I cannot help myself. The goal when I get here becomes gain weight and go home. I am not the only one who feels this way; it is the goal of most of the people here. Most of them, like me, are just here to appease family. There are a few who are here early in their illness, and they might actually have a chance. I hope they can recover before it is too late. I have accepted that this will always be a part of my life. The real question is, "Will I be here to enjoy the rest of my life?" My condition gets worse with every trip. There is more damage done to my organs and other vital systems. Eventually, my body will give up on me too. The bright spots during my "treatment" are the visits that I get from Mom and Sara. I have one coming up and it gives me something to look forward to.

***

Mom and Sara came for a visit, and I had earned a day pass. It simply means that I can be away from the hospital for an entire day without supervision. It feels so good to know that I have earned a privilege. It has been so long since I feel like I have accomplished anything. This is a small victory. I know it is baby steps, but it still makes me feel good.

After talking with Sara and Mom, we decided to go to the zoo. There is a nice zoo close by and Sara is so excited. She loves the zoo, and I know we will spend the entire day there. I try not to think about all the food choices that I will have to make. I will also have to resist the urge to throw up. It is still strong within me, and the only thing that stops me at the hospital is we are monitored in the bathroom. I am a shy person, and the fact that I have someone watch my bathroom activities is both embarrassing and humiliating. Today, however, there will be no monitors, and I will have to resist overeating and throwing up on my own. I tell myself that the staff at the hospital know what they are doing, and they think I am ready for an outing. But there is a part of me that is certain they don't know all my secret thoughts, or the fact that I have the urge to throw up after every meal. I will not tell them because I need this day with my family. I have not been away from the hospital in a while, and it makes me a little stir crazy.

When Sara and Mom arrive, they are given very specific instructions and it makes me feel like a prisoner going on a furlough. Sara can tell that it's making me uncomfortable, so she tries to hurry them along. She will watch me, and she is not afraid to call me on my stuff. Mom listens and asks a ton of questions. Sara is more like me and just wants to get to it. When we finally leave, it feels so strange to be outside the hospital. I have been forbidden to do it for so long it feels like I am doing something wrong. Like I am escaping from prison and Mom and Sara are my rescuers.

The drive to the zoo is spent talking about the family, and everything that is happening at home. I get all the gossip, some good and some bad. That is the thing about living in a small town—we know way too much about our neighbors and they know way too much about us. It is like we never get away from our past. The thought upsets me a little because I want to get away from my past. I want to be a different person, and I can't see that happening in our small town. I am jarred from my musings as we arrive at the zoo. Sara is practically jumping out of her seat. It makes me forget all my problems to see her excitement. I can't remember the last time I was as excited as she is about the zoo. She is so full of life, it is contagious.

The first thing that hits me as we walk through the gates is the aroma of food. All the foods that I love and should not eat. We go by the Food Court quickly, but I am still distracted by the smells. I have a love/hate relationship with food, and the love side of it is hitting me now. It is after I eat that the hate part will take over. Sara sees polar bears, and she pulls me in their direction. Food is forgotten for a moment as she gushes about them.

"Do you want to sit down and watch the polar bears?" I ask.

"You don't mind?" she asks.

I shake my head. She sits down and the look of wonder on her face makes me happy.

The polar bears are very active, and we spend over an hour watching them. I allow her to stay as long as she wants. It is comforting to me to sit here beside her and be normal for a moment. Mom allows us to have this time to ourselves, and she hangs in the background. When we're ready to move on, it is around lunch time and we decide to have hot dogs. I am both incredibly excited and terrified to have a hot dog and fries. The thought of it makes my mouth water, but then the dread of the guilt after hits me. I can see that Mom and Sara are having some anxiety over eating and Mom loudly proclaims that she loves "Nathan's wieners" and it sounds so funny that Sara and I laugh.

"Oh really? Who is Nathan?" I ask, and Sara and I dissolve into fits of giggles. Mom pretends that she is not amused, but I know she loves the fact that we are all together and laughing.

While we are waiting for our order, someone comes up to me and asks if I was on *American Idol*. The person they think I am is handsome, and it makes me feel good. I politely tell them I am not, but I thank them for the compliment.

"You should have told them you were he and charge them for an autograph," Sara teased.

"Exactly," I say, and we both laugh.

I was so thrilled by the compliment that I enjoyed my food with minimal freak outs. After lunch Mom and Sara did not give me a chance to throw up before they whisked me off to the next exhibit. The urge was there, but they distracted me on purpose. It has been so long since I have eaten unhealthy food without throwing it up that my body rebelled a little, and I was only able to make it through half the zoo. My energy level is also very low because I do not get a lot of physical exercise in the hospital. I insisted that Sara finish the zoo. Mom and I sat and had a soda and chatted. Sara saw the rest of the animals alone. She does not mind being alone, and a part of me knows she likes the solitude. I also needed to have Mom time, so it worked out.

The day passed by quickly, and soon it was time to return to the hospital. We all were sad but also encouraged because we had such a good day. It gave me hope for the future. As they walked me back into the hospital, I felt an overwhelming sadness. I did not want them to go. But I also know that I need to stay, as much as I want to be well, this disease is still strong, and I am not ready for home yet.

Chapter 14
Sara

Sadness

My half-sister has been diagnosed with Stage IV breast cancer. I feel numb. The fighter in me wants to believe that she will be fine. I know how much of a fighter she can be. But the medical community does not support my theory. They have told her she does not have much time left. They have also told her how surgery, chemotherapy and radiation will prolong her life. She wants every moment that she can have with her children so she has agreed to try them all. I know it will be hard, but I am proud of her for fighting. She knows that she will not make it, but she is determined to fight for every second of her life.

She has decided that I am in charge of her bucket list and making sure that her children are happy even while she is sick. I have agreed to do whatever I can. She told me I was not allowed to cry or whine. I could not stand over her and have a pity party. She did not want to see one tear from me.

I had to be the one person who treated her in a normal way. If I were in her shoes, I would want the same thing. If I need to cry, then I will do it at home or away from her.

I am so happy that we took the trip to Canada before her illness. I now know why there was a sense of urgency about our trip. This one supervisor at work did not want me to go; now I feel she knows why I defied her. I urge people to follow their gut instincts, and when something feels right, do it. If we had waited it would have been too late. It feels like too much to handle with she and Derrick being sick but I have to try and do all that I can for them. I do not have a choice.

I am also getting a divorce. Why couldn't my husband of twenty-two years wait to do this? His mother is also dying and I have been very active in her care. I make her dinner every night, and she will eat what I cook. I worry that without me she will not eat. However, this was not my choice. He can explain to her why this happened. I don't even understand it myself. He has not just hurt me but also his mom, his children and numerous other people. His selfishness surprises me, and yet I should have expected it. I remember the dream, and I feel sadness. Even in my anger at him, I do not wish him harm. Love does not work that way for me. I do not understand how it works that way for others. But I guess the only emotions I can control are my own, and I am learning day by day to do that.

I have to leave my home because we lived on Sam's family property, and it will be hard to start over. It is the thing that upsets me the most. Having to start all over again. At least, when a person hits rock bottom, the only way to go is up. I have been here before. I will get back up. I will just have to lick my wounds, have a pity party and get over it.

The odd thing is I feel a sense of peace right away. My entire life has been spent answering to other people. Now the only person I have to answer to is myself. I am alone, but there is a power in being alone. I have never been afraid to be by myself. I've always enjoyed those stolen moments of time. The quietness does not bother me, and my anger at the situation keeps the fear at bay. I have always been independent, so I know that financially I will be all right. Starting over is difficult, but I know that I will work hard and restore what has been lost. As much as it hurts, I will survive, and then evolve. I am a firm believer in karma, and Sam will get what he deserves. He is due a ride on the karma train. If I am lucky, maybe I will get to see it. In the meantime, I will concentrate on living well.

Mom and my grandmother drove Derrick to Chapel Hill today. I can tell that he does not want to go, but it is the only way. When he is at the hospital, there is a sense of relief for us. We have hope that he will get better, and for several months, we know that he is safe. But his safety has its price for us.

It is grueling for us when he is there. The facility is four hours away, and we try to visit at least every other week. It is a challenge, both physically and financially. However, I know that Mom will do whatever it takes to help him recover. She also wants him to feel that we are morally supporting him, and that is why she believes the visits are necessary. I have mixed feelings, but I will do what Mom wants. I cannot let her go by herself if I am able to go with her.

When we visit, sometimes we stay the night at the house the hospital has for families. It is very comfortable, and everyone is so nice. Sometimes they let Derrick leave with us for a few hours, and at other times they make us visit at the hospital. It depends on where he is with his treatment. They have a Starbucks at the hospital, and he loves to get coffee from there. When they reward him, they give him a trip to Starbucks. Most people in the program love Starbucks, and I wonder if it is because it is easy to throw up. I don't ask because I never want to dampen the small amount of time we have together. I have learned to pick my battles, and this is not one I need to have. I allow him to have his calorie-laden coffee, knowing in my heart it will come back out. He would never allow himself that many calories without throwing it up. I can tell that Mom is thinking the same thing, but she keeps it to herself as well.

***

They kept Derrick for two months before they deemed him "healed." At this point we know that it is a joke, but one where we all have to play along. There is a part of me that always hopes that this time it sticks, this time everything will be okay. I wonder if Derrick still has that hope? Or has he given up, and he just plays along for our benefit? I know he will not tell me, so I do not ask. We will all just pretend that everything is going to be all right. The holidays are around the corner, and it will be my first one as a single lady.

Divorce can be extremely hard for the holidays, and Derrick recognized that I was struggling. My children are eating with their father on Christmas Day, and I am alone in the afternoon. I know I spent lunch with them and my early morning, but to be alone on Christmas evening feels sad. Derrick suggested we go out. It sounded like a good idea, but there are not any restaurants open on Christmas Day that are worthy of a Christmas meal. Our little town was like a ghost town. Finally, we found a place open, and we decided to try it. It was a small, family restaurant, and we were the only ones there. I felt bad for the staff who had to come in on Christmas Day to serve us, but I was also thankful for them. We ate and laughed the entire time. It was one of those moments that can only be enjoyed with those who know you the best.

Derrick saved me from staying home and wallowing in self-pity. I spent the evening with my little brother, and I will always cherish this memory. He saved me from an evening of tears and ice cream. We made it through this together, and knowing that he loved me enough to do this for me makes my heart swell. I can tell that he had fun as well. We have each other's back, and that is what siblings are for. I know that with his problems, it can be hard at times, but when I really need him, he is there for me. That's what unconditional love is all about.

***

On a happy note, I am going to be a grandmother. I am beside myself because it is a role I have always wanted. My daughter is having a girl in May. Eva, will be a great mom. She has always wanted to have a child, and it is a role she was meant to do. I know there are a lot of people who think they are too young to be a grandmother, and they cringe at the idea, but I am not one of them. When people tease me about being a grandmother, I smile, and I cannot stop smiling. I wonder what she will look like, how she will act. Will she have my personality or Eva's? With all the sad things going on, it adds rays of sunshine into my life. There is hope. Babies are hope for the future.

There are so many negative things, I need a reprieve. Something to get my mind off everything. A mini adventure. I know that right now a big one is out of the question. Even though she is sick, I can tell that Christina has something up her sleeve.

***

My sister dared me to visit my friend Luke.

"I double dare you to visit him," she said to me. We both know that I cannot back down on a double dare.

"I take your dare." I laughed and she smiled.

"You are afraid to visit him," she said, and I shook my head.

"I am fearless, remember?" I said.

"We shall see." It was all she would say. Maybe I was a little afraid. Many people would have been intimidated by the prison and the other inmates, but I knew that the true danger was with my heart. My heart has just started to mend, and I really do not want to rip it open again. There are men whom I know that I will attach myself to and those with whom I know my heart is safe. Luke is the first one, and as much as I want to deny it, it is true. However, I cannot tell my sister this. It would be a sign of weakness, and I am brave.

Luke and I have been corresponding for years. My sister dared me to visit him because she knows how I feel about him. We have experienced a friendship for a very long time, and I was comfortable with the way things were. This would put things outside my comfort zone. I decided to go because she dared me. We have this deal where we always have to complete the dare, no exceptions. To be honest, she knows that I want to go and that I would never do it by myself.

She volunteered to drive me. I was excited about seeing Luke and having a sister day. We had lunch first, but I could barely eat. She noticed but did not tease me. I think she knows I am already nervous.

When we arrived at the prison, I became more nervous, but she told me I was doing this. I started to make an excuse, but it did not work. She practically kicked me out of the truck. I made my way to the line where the visitors were waiting. A lady in line asked me if I had money to buy myself a drink. When I said no, she gave me quarters to buy myself and Luke a drink. I was so thankful for her kindness, and for her presence. She walked me through the process and offered a friendly face in a situation where others are not so friendly. I had only visited a prison as an officer of the court, and going in as a visitor was a different experience.

I checked in and went through the metal detector. One of the women in front of me had on an underwire bra and they made her remove it and go through the detectors before she was allowed to put it back on. If my underwire set off the alarm, I would leave. There was no way I was putting my bra in the container and walking through braless. Luckily, mine did not set the detector off. I went through without issue.

We were all seated at a long table and the inmates had to sit across from us. When Luke walked out, I had a mini panic attack. I was in love with him. All these years of corresponding, I had never allowed myself to have feelings for him. But at that moment I knew. He came over and kissed me, and I was lost. A part of me wanted to run away and never look back. I knew if I stayed for that entire visit, I would be hooked. I could never leave him again, alone. The logical person inside of me said that I cannot love someone in prison; that would be crazy. The entire visit I had face sweats and felt I could not breathe. He was calm and sweet, everything I imagined him to be. He was hot and I was a hot mess. He pretended not to notice my craziness. I could only imagine what he was thinking. He probably could not wait for me to leave. However, he just sat there with the most incredible smile on his face. When the two-hour visit was over, he kissed me again. I did not want it to ever end. I felt a bit wanton for allowing him such a deep kiss, for allowing myself to get lost in the moment. It was as if we were the only two people in the room. I lost myself in him, and I felt as if he did the same with me.

"Will you come back?" he asked.

"Yes," was all I could say. I left the prison with complete happiness. I wanted to skip to the truck. I could not wipe the smile off my face. I knew Christina would notice, and a part of me did not care.

When I got back to the truck, my sister started laughing.

"What?" I asked.

"You are in love with him," she said with a smile.

"No way. That would be crazy," I said, but I was not convincing. My big, goofy, smile gave me away.

"You're in love with someone in prison, and now I will be the favorite," she said with a giggle.

Sadness

"I will find a way to make it all your fault," I said, and we both laughed. The scary thing was, she was right. I loved him. I had never allowed myself to have feelings for him outside of friendship. The cynic in me told me I was insane, but the butterflies in my stomach, were much more convincing. One's head can tell you many things, but it is not a match for the heart and butterflies in the stomach.

You make
me
bloom

Chapter 15
Derrick

Still Obsessed

I AM HOME again, but I don't know how long I will be. I am not well. The food obsessions are all still there, and most of the weight I have gained is just swelling that will go down quickly. I want to be home, but it would be better to be home healed and whole. My mom and sister know that I am not well. They tried to get the doctors to keep me, but the hospital has to follow the protocol that the insurance sets. They believe if my weight is within the guidelines, then I am fine. Nothing could be further from the truth.

My father wants to come see me, but a part of me just wants to be done with him. When I say this, many people lecture me. But just because he was my sperm donor, does not mean he was ever a father to me. He only wants to come around when he has a new woman and wants to show her what a family man he is to me. It is a joke. I do not want to be a part of it. For my entire life, he has either ignored me or been emotionally abusive.

He was never supportive or encouraging. He never misses an opportunity to let me know what a failure I am.

As if I care what he thinks. At one time I did, and I wanted to be the person that could make him proud, but that is an impossibility. It is he and not I. He is an angry and bitter person, and I don't have the time nor the energy to try and understand him. He will blame Mom because I do not want to visit, but it is my decision. It is one less thing to deal with. He has never visited me when I go to the hospital at Chapel Hill or when I go to our local hospital. He told me once that he drove up, but there was no parking. The hospital always has empty spaces, but I did not argue with him. It is easier if he thinks I believe his lies.

My immediate family visits on a regular basis. I know they want me to be well, and they try to encourage me. At times I just want to be myself because as much as they love me, they will never understand. An eating disorder is all consuming, and as much as I love them, I don't have the energy for all their questions. My family is at my home a lot, and I have become accustomed to their presence.

Sean is always visiting me, and so is Eva. They are more like my siblings in many ways. Sean and I are only a little over a year apart. We all grew up together, and I know it is hard for them to see me this way. I cannot imagine how I would feel if the roles were reversed. The thought nauseates me. I would rather it be I, than they. I would not wish this hell on anyone, much less the ones I love.

My extended family is also very supportive. There are fifty of us, and we are all close. Anyone who messes with one of us, will have all of us to deal with. They were not aware of the bullying, or they would have tried to help, just like Sara and Mom.

My sister has a lot going on. She is going through a divorce, and her half-sister has cancer. They grew up together and are very close. I know that Sara is devastated but cannot do anything about it.

A bright spot is that Eva is having a baby, and that is very exciting. We are all already in love with the baby, and she is not even here yet. Eva did a 3D ultrasound, so we got a peek at her. Mom and I talk about how we can watch her when Eva returns to work. I feel a new baby will give me purpose and help me focus on something besides throwing up.

Sara has also gone to visit her friend, Luke, in prison. I know this sounds like a bad thing on the surface, but in reality, I think it is good. Luke has been a friend to her, and she could use a friend right now. She seems smitten with him, even though she denies it vehemently. I just want her to be happy. If she finds joy with him, I will be happy for her.

I have written Luke a letter or two because I want to get to know him. I would never want to visit him at the prison because that is too stressful. All those people staring at me . . . and the fences and bars . . . the very idea freaks me out. I will just have to get to know him through letters. He seems to be a nice guy.

I cannot believe that Eva is all grown up and is about to have a child. She has grown up too fast. I remember several years ago going to Georgia to pick her up at a friend's place. Sara and I went together, and I drove. Driving has always made me nervous, and I was proud of myself for taking the trip. We went to get off at an exit to have dinner. I was happy that I had made it so far without a nervous breakdown. Sara kept giving me positive reinforcement. We were chatting away when a truck stopped suddenly in front of me. I tried to stop but my brakes did not catch. We rammed into the truck in front of us.

When I came to, Sara and I were in the car and the air bags had deployed. I could smell smoke.

"I think we should get out," Sara said in a dazed voice.

"We should," I said, but neither of us moved. It was as if our brains could not communicate with our bodies.

"I think the car is on fire," Sara said. I looked up and I could see smoke coming from the hood area. We still sat in the car and did not move.

"It is definitely on fire," I said, and we finally moved. Getting out of the car was difficult because the air bags were in the way, and we were sore. I am sure we looked crazy climbing out of the car in slow motion. The guy in the truck told us we needed to get away from the car because it was on fire, so we allowed him to usher us away. When we were away from the car and safe, we started to process what had happened. The driver in the truck was very nervous. He had already called 911 so we were just waiting on them to come. The driver of the truck was frantically throwing things in a garbage can nearby. Now I knew why he was so nervous they were beer cans. I wasn't sure why he was afraid, and now I knew. He had been drinking. I nudged Sara. She watched him with me. The wreck was not his fault, it was the fault of my brakes that went out, and I wanted to tell him to calm down. But observing him trying to cover his tracks was so amusing, Sara and I continued to watch him, in between watching the front of my car burn up. We were both quiet, seeing the chaos around us as though we were not a part of the craziness, just bystanders. The police and firemen, showed up and put out the fire. I did not get a ticket because my brakes were faulty. They were what was causing the fire. We did not tell on the drunk guy in the truck. I had been the drunk guy before, so no judgment from me. After the drama was all over, we were stranded. Sara called Eva, and she and her friend agreed to pick us up. The only thing nearby was the restaurant we were planning to eat at when we got off the exit. Sara told me to call Mom about the accident and see if she could drive to pick us up. Eva's friend could only take us the thirty minutes to their house; they could not drive us the four-hour distance to our house. When I called Mom, she said she could not pick us up. I got off the phone, and I know I had a weird look on my face.

"When is she coming?" Sara asked.

"She's not," I said, still a bit in shock.

"What do you mean she is not coming?" she said, and I laughed.

"She said she can't come and get us," I said. "And she told me to get her golf clubs out of the trunk of the car." Sara looked so shocked it made me laugh. When she saw me laughing, she started laughing. We were both standing there on the side of the road in a small town in Georgia, laughing hysterically. When we finally got over our laughter, we dragged the golf clubs out of the trunk... with all our other stuff, Sara takes books everywhere, so we were loaded down, and we went to wait on Eva at the Country Western restaurant.

When we walked in the wait staff tried not to react even though I am pretty sure we looked crazy. Sara was in a mood by then, so I was happy no one said anything. We ordered and ate like nothing had happened until Eva showed up. She had also called her dad and he was coming to pick us up. She had spoken to Mom. Mom had said, "It isn't that I won't come get you, I'm just not sure my car will make the trip."

At that point, Sara and I did not care. We had a ride home and food in our belly. We would worry about the rest tomorrow.

CHAPTER 16
Sara

Changes

WHEN THEY LET Derrick come home, even the physicians said, "This time, he needs to stay. Unfortunately, the insurance will not pay once he gains a certain amount of weight," they explained sadly. So they sent him home. He was not home very long before we had to take him back to the hospital. He went to our local hospital, because he was too sick to make it to Chapel Hill. It infuriates me that with all the medical advancements there is nothing they can do for him. The clinicians at the local hospital suggest a feeding tube, but he has made it clear that he would not tolerate it. He is also his own guardian, so it is his choice. He does not want to be fed through a feeding tube, and we cannot force it upon him. If something does not happen soon, I know that he will die.

My daughter had a baby the night that Derrick almost died. I was in the hospital with Eva while my mom was in a hospital an hour away with Derrick slipping away. His blood pressure dropped to a dangerous level, and we transferred to ICU. I would go out in the hall and call my mom to check on Derrick. I know that she was devastated. I could not be there for my mom and all I could do was pray for him and her. I also had to hide Derrick's plight from Eva, and that was difficult as well. He stabilized before Jade was born, so I could relax a bit. Sam, Eva's father, was there for the birth, and he was very supportive. It seems we have forged a friendship, and I believe that is important for our children, and now our grandchildren.

Jade was born healthy and happy, and I was so delighted that for a moment I was able to forget Derrick's illness and everything that went with it. I was in the room when she was born and it was the most amazing experience of my life. She brings hope and love to our family during a time when we are all struggling. Mom came up to see her as soon as she could. From the moment she saw her, she loved her as I did. She will give us all the sunshine that we need.

***

In the midst of all the craziness with Derrick, and the birth of Jade, I decide to marry Luke. There are so many people who have opinions on what I should or should not do concerning him, I decide to only share this news with my immediate family. I did not want someone with a negative opinion to ruin this day. My mind is made up, and they are not going to change it. I tell Eva, Sean, my mom and Christina. Eva went with me to the prison. I was a nervous wreck for a variety of reasons. When we arrive, everyone is uncharacteristically jovial. They are not as strict about the check-in procedure as they are when I visit. We go into the visitation area, and I meet the minister. We are lucky enough to have the man who introduced us serve as our minister. It makes things feel right, as if fate brought us to this point. I talk to the minister for a bit while they are getting Luke. Eva is trying to keep me calm because she can tell that I am extremely nervous. All my worries slip away when Luke comes out. His smile lights up the room. He comes over, grabs me and gives me a huge hug. I feel a sense of relief in his endearment.

"I didn't think you would show up," he says and I smile. The thought of not showing up had never occurred to me.

"I would never do that to you," I say and kiss him.

"Save that for after," the minister jokes and we all laugh.

He starts the ceremony, and I read my vows first. I stumble over them in my nervousness. I can see tears in Luke's eyes, and it makes it even harder to speak. I never thought I would do this again and yet here I am. Eva is snapping pictures as I talk. It all seems like a dream.

By the time he finishes his vows, I have tears in my eyes as well. The vows are beautiful, everything that I want to hear. He says all the things that I feel. The minister even seems touched. He pronounces us husband and wife, and then Eva and the minister leave. Eva had brought a book to amuse herself in the car. She knows that we will have this time together.

We are allowed two, blissful hours together. It is everything that I wanted it to be. The fact that he had put so much thought into his vows, into this moment, makes me feel loved, more than I have ever been by a man. He is my other half, and I know it. He is my husband; I am his wife.

After the two hours, it is difficult to leave. I want to take him home with me. It is sad that I have to leave, but I had braced myself for this so I do not shed a tear. I know in my heart that he is my soulmate. The one that God put on this earth for me.

As we pull away from the prison, I cry both happy and sad tears. I am married to someone in prison. If someone had told me years ago that I would be married to someone in prison, I would have laughed. Today it feels like the most natural thing in the world, and I cannot imagine being married to anyone else. I love him, and he loves me, and the rest will work itself out. I can only imagine the things people will say. Most people will never understand, and it is difficult to explain to them. I really cannot explain love.

When I arrive at home, I decide to go kayaking. I need a moment to process the day's events before I let the world in. I know that there are many people who will be negative, and I need the tranquility of kayaking so I can enjoy the moment. I can't wait to bring Luke with me. To have him enjoy something that I love so much. My mind drifts to things we will share when he gets out. All the things that we have to look forward to in the future. He is my future and my happily-ever-after. I know that it is also hard on Luke to be alone, so I hope he finds a way to enjoy the rest of his wedding day.

I come in from kayaking, ready to take on the criticism of the world. I fall asleep talking to Luke, with the smell of him, river water and sunshine on my skin. The perfect ending to a day that will shape the rest of my life.

I cannot believe that I became a grandmother this year, got married and I am in charge of my sister's bucket list. My sister, her family and I have been swimming with dolphins, kayaking with manatees (where we also skinny dipped, or chunky dunked with them), hunting for shark's teeth, making numerous beach trips, enjoying Disney, Sea World, having dinner with Shamu and experiencing a variety of other things. My sister has been sick for most the trips that we have taken. She has been through chemotherapy, radiation and surgery. However, she still insists on going and spending quality time with her family.

Chapter 17
Derrick

New Life

My niece just had a baby, and I am crazy about her. She makes everything right in the world. I have decided to stop drinking. If I cannot do it for myself, then I will do it for her.

I have made a new commitment and it is as follows:

> Oh God, I am a sinner. I am sorry for my sin. I now turn to Jesus for forgiveness, and I thank you for what you have done for me through him. I received Jesus into my heart, and I want him to be the Lord of my life. I want to follow him in fellowship of the church. Take charge of me, Lord. Help me in my problems. Lift the burdens of my heart. Make a new person out of me. In Jesus name, I pray. Amen.

I went to the altar at church this morning, and I prayed for God to help me stop drinking. I cried and had everyone pray with me. I am a very private person and the fact that I went to the altar at all shows how much that I want this. I know God is the only one who can help me. I cannot give this up by myself. I am too weak. But I know he can help me with this battle, and with his help, I can win.

My mom is so excited and hopeful. She believes in me, and she wants me to succeed. Her hope for me gives me hope for the future. Knowing I have someone on my side makes me stronger. With her and God, how can I help but conquer this demon? I feel it in my soul that I can stop with God on my side. It feels good to be able to do something positive for myself and my family.

Mom and I watch Jade while Eva works, and it makes me so happy. She is brand new and has her entire life ahead of her. I want to teach her all the things that she needs to know. I want her to be strong and brave. I never want her to endure the bullying that I had to endure. She is my hope and my strength. Her birth has helped me conquer my addiction to alcohol. It is strange that such a tiny person can change my life in such a drastic way.

The flip side of me not drinking is that all my focus goes to the eating disorder. It is the one thing I cannot seem to give up no matter how hard I try. I believe I still relate it to the bullying. I have to be skinny. I can never be fat again, and this is the only way to assure myself I will not gain the weight back.

My family has told me about the night Jade was born and how I almost died. I don't remember most of it because I was out of it. I feel deep regret that I was not there with Eva and that Mom could not be there because of me. It breaks my heart. I have to dedicate my life to doing better to make it up to her. Giving up alcohol is a part of that. I wish I could commit to giving up the rest, but I am not ready to let it go. I still need it.

Chapter 18
Sara

Babies and Marriage

JADE HAS MADE Derrick stop drinking. It is a miracle and an answer to prayers. I can tell that my mom is so relieved. Jade has taken something away from him, the desire to drink, that hurt my mom. He was so different when he was drinking. He was not himself. Even though there were times when he was funny, sometimes he was belligerent and cruel. This is a step in the right direction for him. The fact that he has stopped gives us all hope for the future.

Luke and I are doing well. We have settled into a pattern of letters, phone calls and visits. It is not an easy relationship, but it works for us. Most people do not understand, and I do not feel the need to explain it to them. If I have learned anything in the last several years, it is I do not have to explain myself to anyone. My days for giving people an explanation about my life and choices are over. I have made my own way, and I am proud of the fact that I have remained strong, even in hard times. People never know how strong they can be until challenges are handed to them, such that strong is the only choice.

My visits with Luke are so intense. I have never felt this way. When we are together, I forget that I am in a room full of people and that some of them are watching us. I can't get enough of his touch, his kiss and his love for me. When he looks at me I feel like I am the most beautiful girl in the world, and like I am the only person in the room. People at visitation even comment about the way we are toward one another. It makes me happy that they can see how we feel about one another. There are so many of my friends and family who have not seen us together. They do not understand. It is nice to have people who can see it and comprehend our connection.

Sam remarried shortly after I did. His new wife does not want his children around, and he does not push the issue. I do not know the person he has become. I wonder what the boy I married would think about the man he has become. I don't even feel anger anymore. Just sadness. It frustrates me, but there is little I can do about it. When it comes to him, I have to let go of the hate and vindictiveness. I leave it to God and karma.

My sister is getting worse. I wish there was something I could do to save her. Even though she does not openly discuss her condition with me, I see the decline. It is my job to keep the children happy, and I know she is worse when I go over and find she wants me to take them somewhere. When I go over, that request is occurring more frequently. She does not like me to see her when she is having a bad day, and I know that she does not want the children to see it either. She is sparing us from seeing her pain, but that does not mean that I don't know and can't see how much pain she is in. I allow her to shield me, but I know.

I can tell when she feels well because she wants me to talk about our future trips. It brings her joy. These pockets of time when we can go somewhere as a family help her through the hard times. I can see her light up when we talk about what we are going to do. She has always loved a great adventure, and it is the one thing I can do for her and her family. We have several fun things coming up, and I hope she is well enough to do them. I know the trips are hard on her in some ways, but they also seem to give her strength.

I think that quality of life is very important, and these trips add quality to her life and the lives of her children. It gives them good memories of happy times. I hope that at the end of my life, I will have a love for life so much that I do not stop living it until the end.

The correlation between her and Derrick is not lost to me. I feel like Derrick has never started to

Babies and Marriage

live. His life has been centered around fear, and he will not put himself out there. I want him to have the same fight for life as Christina, but it seems impossible. It is not in his nature. The thought makes me sad.

CHAPTER 19
Derrick

Last Trip to the Beach

I AM GOING to try Chapel Hill again. Mom has promised that when I complete the program, she will take Sara and me to the beach. Even though the beach is not my favorite place, going there with Mom and Sara appeals to me. We never really have time, just the three of us, unless it is driving me to treatment or going to treatment meetings. It will be nice to just have fun with the three of us. It will also motivate me to gain weight faster. I know how to gain the weight quickly now, and I also know how to lose it just as fast. It is a deadly game that I play, but I can't seem to stop.

I completed the program again and Mom is taking me and Sara to the beach. I have decided to enjoy this time with my mom and sister. I want this to be a memorable trip for all of us. A part of me wonders if this will be the last time I see the ocean. I am under no illusions about how sick I really am. Mom feels the same way. I can see it in her eyes. This trip will be bittersweet for all of us.

Sara loves the ocean, the water; it has always been part of her. She attacks it with the same enthusiasm that she does everything else. I love her vibrancy and joy for life. I live vicariously through her in many ways.

She also seems happy with her marriage to Luke. I think a part of her likes that he is not here but tucked safely away. It allows her certain freedoms that her previous marriage denied her. She has created a life for herself, and she is not afraid to be alone. When people ask her about being alone, she always tells them, "You are only lonely if you do not like the person you are alone with." She reiterates that she is happy with herself. I admire and envy her for that.

When we get to the condo, Sara allows me to pick the room. I pick the back one and let her have the one from which she can see the ocean from the bed. Her smile makes it all worth it. I know that is the one she wanted.

I am trying so hard not to obsess about food, but it is a struggle. It was difficult to go to the grocery store to buy breakfast, lunch and snack items. I was very stressed out when we left the store, and it was pretty apparent. Sara smoothed it over and after she quickly put up the groceries, she suggested a walk on the beach. I love to pick up shells and sea glass, so I agreed. I also needed to get away from the food. I wanted to eat it all, and then throw it up. The urge to do it was only taken away by the walk on the beach and the knowledge that it would hurt Sara and Mom.

After the walk on the beach, Sara convinced Mom and I to get in the hot tub with her. This required a swimsuit, and I had several small breakdowns before I put it on and followed Sara to the hot tub. Sara knew I was freaking out, so we walked quickly and did not hesitate getting in. Once I was in the tub, I could allow myself to be swallowed with the bubbles. Sara took pictures of me and Mom, and I did not freak out about how they might look. I let her take them, and we laughed and made funny faces. Mom even got into it and laughed so hard she was almost crying. It felt so normal and fun that I forgot about food for a time and just enjoyed myself. It was a moment that I will always remember, and I am happy that Sara convinced me to go outside of my comfort zone.

After the hot tub, we went back to the condo and got ready for dinner. We were all craving seafood, and there are a ton of places on the beach to eat. We chose one on the water where we watched the birds perch on the dock as we ate. An occasional dolphin jumped, and Sara would squeal with glee every time we saw one. It was a magical day. I did not throw up the entire day, and even though I knew it could not last, at least I was able to give that gift of one day to Sara and Mom, and to myself.

The next day was a little more difficult. After gorging on bagels and cream cheese for breakfast,

I had to throw it all up. When I came out of the bathroom, Sara and Mom knew, but they did not confront me. It was as if they wanted this trip so much that they would even tolerate the binging and vomiting. We spent the morning at the beach. I did not wear my swimsuit, but at least I sat on the beach in shorts and a t-shirt. It was nice to talk to Sara and Mom and watch the people go by. Sara played in the waves, and her laughter made me happy. If only I could be so carefree. Mom read and did not get in the water, but she enjoyed the time she spent with us. She just looked happy, and I wish I could give her happier moments and fewer sad ones. The guilt is overwhelming at times, but today I will not allow it to send me into a downward spiral.

For the remainder of the trip, I attempted to stay jovial. I had occasional relapses, but I recovered faster than normal.

We all needed this trip, and I will not mess it up, I determined. *I have messed up too much already.* When the time came to leave, I was sad. I could tell that Mom and Sara were as well. This feels like the last time that we will see the ocean together and the finality of it rips through me.

It should encourage me to change and to get better, but I am not sure that's in the cards for me. I wish I could do it, if not for myself, then for Mom and Sara. I'm just not sure that I can.

I am not "healed" as they would have me believe when the Chapel Hill team released me from the hospital. I have accepted the fact that I will never get well. I have not told anyone; I can't take their hope away. In a way, I believe Sara and Mom already know, and that is one reason they insisted on this trip.

Chapter 20
Sara

A New Hurt

DERRICK FINISHED ANOTHER session at Chapel Hill, and Mom is taking us to the beach. I think in many ways, she feels like this might be her last chance to take us together. Derrick is not getting better. I am excited about the trip. It is the only time that just the three of us have gone to the beach alone.

When we picked Derrick up, it was obvious that he was not well. He was swollen with fluid and had made the goal weight so he could go home. I think that he has learned to beat the system, and part of that is doing things that make him swell so he will weigh more. I refrained from commenting. The swelling will go down, and he will weigh less, and that is what he really wants. As soon as we got to the car, he had already started talking about the fact that he looked pudgy and losing a few pounds would not hurt. Mom and I didn't say anything because we knew it would do little good. We wanted this beach trip to go well.

When we arrived, the condo was right on the beach, and it was beautiful. Mom was happy, and I could tell that Derrick was really trying hard to enjoy himself. I talked him into a walk on the beach. As we walked, we picked up sea glass. The way we picked up sea glass said a lot about our personalities. I picked up every piece that appealed to me. It did not have to be perfect. I had a bag full quickly. However, Derrick only wanted to pick up perfect pieces. If he saw a flaw, he discarded it. When I picked up a perfect piece, I gave it to him. If only he could learn to love imperfections, I thought. Then he would love himself more. I guess the sea glass is how we feel about ourselves. I love the broken parts of me, the imperfections. They are what make me unique, and I would not change them. However, Derrick wants perfection, so he only keeps the perfect parts. It is hard for anyone to strive for perfection, and it often leaves disappointment. I just want him to be happy, with all the parts of him.

After we finished our walk, we went to the pool. It took me lots of pleading to get Derrick in a bathing suit, but I succeeded. Even though he still wore his t-shirt I was happy he was going to the pool with me. Mom, Derrick and I spent the evening in the pool and hot tub. We laughed and joked more than we had in years. We even had seafood at a local restaurant without major food drama.

The next day Derrick took too much of his medication by accident, and although he was amusing, it was not the day we had planned. We managed some time on the beach, and we had dinner in the condo. His food obsessions have returned, or they never left. He is writing down every morsel he eats and obsessing over it. I have not heard him throw up, but it is a hard thing to monitor. I suspected that he threw up after breakfast, but I did not push the issue. A part of me wants to stay here in our bubble. Maybe here I can protect him, but I know that is not true. He has to save himself and be the hero of his own story. As hard as I've tried, I can't do it for him.

When we finally packed the car and left, I felt sad. Somehow, I believe we will never go on another vacation together again. This will be it, if he does not get better. The thought hurts me. We laugh and cut up on the way home. It's like we all know we need to cherish every moment. Reality will hit us soon enough.

***

When I return to work, I have a ton of messages from Scott. He knows that he is not supposed to contact me. He was shipped away because his guardian thought I was in danger from him. Before they shipped him, he showed up at my office and held me inside for an hour. A coworker had to call the police, and the next day our building was vandalized with phrases targeted at me. They shipped him, but I fear it was not far enough. As negative as it sounds, I don't know if it will ever be far enough. He has stalked me for years, and it is only a matter of time before he finds me again. I call his case manager, and report the calls and crazy messages. They document everything, and they assure me they will do all they can to keep me safe. I feel a chill, because I know their best will not be good enough.

***

Scott finds me after months of stalking me. I knew it would happen eventually, but I could never really prepare myself. I just open my door at home one day to leave and there he is.

"Honey, I'm home," he says.

I know I will have to fight for my life, but not with my fists. I could never beat him in a fight. He alludes to the fact that he has a knife. I see the bulge in his pocket and I believe him.

I try so hard to stay calm while he hurts me. Every time I struggle, he chokes me, and I know to struggle means to die. He would have no problem killing me. I have to talk him out of it even through my panic. "If you kill me, they will know it is you. It will be easier to let me go."

It takes all my strength to cooperate with him. I will have to remove myself from the situation, forget the pain and degradation and concentrate on living. But it is my instinct to fight . . . but fighting will not benefit me . . . so I succumb . . . I remove myself from the situation.

I talk him into letting me take him back to his group home. "Let me drive you back to Candler. I promise you I will never tell. It will be our secret." Promises I will never keep, but I only have to convince him. In his mind we are in love and meant to be together. While we are driving, he touches me and gets my hand and touches himself. It takes all I have not to jerk my hand away. I want to vomit, but I have to act normal. It is the only thing that will save me, and I know it. If he suspects that he has nothing to lose, he will kill me.

I take him to the group home and walk him in. I get away as soon as possible. The creepy group manager gives me a smile, and in my mind I know he helped him get to me. I think he allowed this to happen, and if I felt stronger, I would have told him. However, all I want to do is get back to my car and lock the door.

When I get to my car, I crumble. I manage to drive to my mom's house. I call one of my friends from work on the way home. She manages to understand what has happened even through my hysteria. She tells me she will call my mom and daughter and tell them what happened so that I will not have to talk about it anymore for the day. I cannot deal with rehashing things with them or with anyone.

Everyone tries so hard to act normal, and Derrick is so supportive. When I truly need him, he is there for me. I know at the end of the day he always has my back. It gives me comfort.

Scott has been in trouble before and because of his IQ, he was allowed to go free. I know that having him arrested will not stick. He uses his disability to assault women. He has been doing this for years without any real repercussions. The court system will just put him where he is now. He is already in a home for sexual predators. I have little recourse.

***

I get up the next morning and go to work. I do not want to sit at Mom's house all day and relive things. When I arrive at work, someone asks me how I'm doing, and I start crying. I continue to cry while I work. There is a man there who is doing remodeling work. No one has told him what has occurred. He calls my boss and tells her I am crying and that he is worried about me. She comes and picks me up and takes me to a counselor and to the police station. It is useless to have him arrested because he has done this before and was not charged because of his disability. His IQ is low enough to be considered mentally retarded, but I suspect that he fudged the test. He is smarter than he has tested, but I do not have the ability to fight him on this issue. The police suggested a stalking order because it will keep him away from me, and it will add some accountability to the group home. They are supposed to be a secured facility, and they will have consequences now if he gets to me. I complete the paperwork and I feel empowered.

After, I make sure everything is secure. I have the stalking order in place, and I have numbers to call if I see him. I decide to go home for the night. I cannot stay with Mom forever, and I believe it is easier to face things than to run from them. I go home and clean up everything. Cleaning up is difficult because it brings back ugly memories, but I manage to do it alone. I can't have anyone here to help or watch. I handle things better by myself. I will not allow him to make me run from my home. A friend comes and installs some alarms for me. I never thought alarms were necessary in my small hometown. I believed locks were enough. Now I know that it is not safe without them.

I talk to my neighbors about the issue. They are very supportive, and I know they will keep a watch out for strangers. I put a baseball bat beside my bed and go to sleep. If he comes again, I will be ready for him. I will not live in fear. I will not allow him to steal my peace from me.

I know I have to tell Christina. Even though she is sick, she will want to know. I have never been able to hide things from her. I go over and climb into bed with her. My stepmom had given her the basics of the situation. I hate to see the pity in her eyes.

"Don't look at me like that; it's not like I have cancer or anything," I say and give her a small smile. This is our dark humor, and I know it.

"Yeah. I always have to one-up you," she says, and she tries to smile, but it does not reach her eyes. I don't want her to be sad for one minute on my behalf. She has enough to worry about.

"Do you want me to kick his ass?" she asks, and I shake my head, trying hard not to cry. I know she means it; even sick, she would fight for me.

"We will let karma get him," I say, and she does not argue. Instead we watch a movie and talk about all the places we want to go. It is what we do. Life is too short to wallow in self-pity. We suck it up and move on.

find joy
in your
trials
because
they build
patience

Chapter 21
Derrick

Endings Are Sad

I am going to Chapel Hill again, and we all know this will be the last time. They have said very clearly that this is my last chance. Mom and Sara are going to drive me. I know that I am in bad condition and they are worried about the trip. Sara is trying to be positive, but I see past the smile. She knows that this is going to be bad, and it is hard for even her to smile and be happy.

I am really sick, and to be honest, I go in and out. I only remember tidbits of the drive to Chapel Hill. I know we stop to eat and get out at several rest areas, but I cannot remember anything about it. I just remember Mom and Sara helping me in and out of the car. I have vague memories of them taking me into the bathroom. I block those memories because they are too humiliating. I have always been modest, and the thought of them seeing me in the bathroom makes me feel horrible.

Mom asks, "Do you want to call your dad?"

"I do not." He has not been around in a while, and I have no regrets. He has chosen this path with our relationship, and I do not have the energy to mend it. As selfish as it sounds, I hope he feels guilt for what he has done to our family. I have done nothing to make it bad, so I will not spend my last days trying to fix it. What is done is done. It will be his burden soon, if he cares at all.

I spend several days in the ICU before I am allowed to go into the normal program. I am still weak when I get there, and I can tell that everyone is extremely worried about me. I have completed this program so many times that I jump into it with gusto. I just want to get it finished and go home. I could write the program myself. When the counselors talk in group, I can almost finish their sentences. It isn't the knowledge that I lack, it is the incentive for change. I am not ready to give up this addiction. I have allowed it to consume my life, and there is no going back. I will complete this program again and go home; there will not be another time here. I know deep inside what that means, and I am ready to accept the consequences of that decision. However, I keep this to myself because more than anything I want to go home.

***

Finally, they have deemed me well enough to go home. We all know it is a joke, but we pretend that everything is just peachy. Sara and Mom pick me up. They are happy for me to come home, but they know, as I do, I am not cured. I am swollen, and I do not look well. I hate the swelling, but it is part of the way that I can come home quickly and then lose it quickly. Swelling is part of the Russian Roulette game that I play with my life.

***

This creep hurt Sara. I feel so helpless. I wonder if this is how she feels all the time with me. I hate to see her broken and hurt. She is strong, and I know what it would take to break her. She does not want to talk about it, and this is the one thing I understand. Every time Mom tries to say something about it, I shut her down. I have to protect Sara. Even though I can't make it go away, I can prevent anyone from making her relive every moment. She smiles at me. She knows what I am doing.

It is hard to see her afraid. I can see her fighting her fears. When she tells us she is going back to her house where it happened, I panic a bit. But I also understand her need to face her fears head-on and quickly. It is her personality. I can tell that Mom wants her to stay, but I know Sara and she will not agree. She has to be in charge of her own life, and she will not allow anyone to take that away from her.

Mom and I offer to go home with her, but she refuses. It is something that she has to do alone. We want to clean up, to make the house better for her, but she insists on doing it herself. Sadly, we watch her go, and mom tells her to call us later and let us know how she is doing. I already know what she will say. She will say that she is fine even though nothing could be further from the truth. We have this in common. Because I am fine too. We can call that line fiction but painfully true.

CHAPTER 22
Sara

An Adventure End

Mom and I drove Derrick to Chapel Hill today. He was almost comatose on the way down. I had so much anxiety taking him down. I really thought he would not live through the trip. The thought of him dying in the car with us gave me mini panic attacks, and I know that Mom felt the same way. I tried to think of what we would do if he coded. Would we call an ambulance? Try to drive him to the closest hospital? All I could concentrate on was getting him to the hospital at Chapel Hill as quickly as possible. I wanted him to be in more capable hands than mine. I wanted him to be safe.

We even had to stop and change him because he soiled himself. I know it is bad when he does not protest Mom and me stripping him and changing him. He barely reacted. Mom looked at me and we both knew it was serious. He had been sick before, but this was different. This seemed like the end, and the thought caused ripples of pain through me. I was not ready; he was not ready.

When we got him there, he was in critical condition and had to be put in the ICU to get better before he could be admitted into the program. They did not allow Mom and me to stay with him. He was that sick. We had to drive the four hours home, leaving him there. We prayed all the way home.

***

Luckily Derrick stabilized over the next few days and was allowed to go into the regular program. They have informed us this is his last chance. They will not take him again. In our hearts, we knew this, but hearing it said is still hard. This is his last chance. This reverberates through my head. It has a finality to it that scares me. Somehow knowing that this is his last chance frightens me more than ever. There will be no more trips to Chapel Hill. No more peace when he is there. He has to get better this time. He cannot die. My heart cannot take it. My sister is dying too. They cannot die.

***

My sister passes away. She waits until I leave her house. I had been there for a long time, and then when I leave, she lets go. I know she did not want me to see her that way. Even in death she spares me. The thought brings me sadness. I wanted to be there for her, but I also understand her reasoning. We were always about life, the two of us; it was our connection. Dying is not what she wanted me for; I was in charge of her living, and my job was done. There will be no more adventures for us.

After months of bucket-list adventures, it is her time. She fought so hard, right up until the end. She passes away at home, as she wanted. And she waits until I leave to die as she wants. Maybe she knew that it was the one thing I could not see. I was in denial that she would die, right up until the last. I refused to accept it. I thought if I gave up, she would too. I think that is why she waited. She knew I was in denial.

Her children will need me, and in an odd way, I will need them as well. The only way to survive her loss is together. Her husband is lost as well, and my dad and stepmom are devastated. It is hard to recover from this kind of loss. How can we go on without her? I do not have that answer.

Her funeral is on the rocks of the river where we played as a child. It was our spot. I remember we always told Dad that it was our land. He said it was, and I requested the deed. He laughed. "You will have to trust me. I will give it to you two." I suppose my trust issues started early.

Her funeral is all the things she wanted. She wanted to be in the river with her baby that passed years before. We all gather there together and sing hymns, I read a poem that my friend Barb wrote for her, and we put her ashes in the river, as she had requested. I break down as I read the poem, and Dad and Sam come to stand by me. I finish it even through my tears. I need to do it for her. She would do the same for me. Everyone puts flowers in the river as well. We linger as the flowers drift. I have a strong urge to grab a kayak and follow them down. However, I know that her children need me. We have guests to console us, and I have to be there to help everyone handle everything. I feel like a part of me is floating down the river with her. I follow the flowers as they float in the river. I follow them as far as I can go, and then I allow them to drift through the culvert.

Sam was standing there waiting on me when I walked up the river bank.

"I'm sorry," he says, lingering as if he wants to say more.

"I know. Me too," I say.

He looks miserable.

"I'll be fine," I say. "You can go. It isn't your job to comfort me anymore" Before he can interrupt, I continue. "It is okay. I promise," I assure him and he hugs me. Then he turns and leaves. Christina would be proud of me. She always knew that I did not need him. I talk to the guests and the children play in the yard. I think of my promise to Christina that we will stay a family. It will not be an easy promise, but I know it was important to her, and to me. After everyone leaves, Christina's husband sits by the river, and her children have settled nearby. It is time for me to take some time for my grief.

***

I went kayaking in Christina's honor today. I went alone and talked to her. It sounds a little crazy, but I did. Every place on the river holds a memory of her. As I meandered down the river, I stopped and reminisced about our adventures. The river had always been a part of us. When we were children, we made it our life's goal to swim every chance we got. In the winter months, one of us "accidently" fell in, and then the other one had to jump in for the rescue. It was what we did, so this day it was what I chose to do. I laughed, cried and went skinny dipping or chunky dunking. It is what she would have wanted. I felt she was there with me; her spirit followed me. When I arrived at the boat dock, the smell of river water and sunshine lingered on my skin. Christina always said if we could bottle that smell, we could make millions. It is truly the best smell in the world. However, maybe it was just our smell, and I know that everyone does not like it as much as we did. I felt the tears on my cheeks, and tasted the saltiness of them as they flowed down my face.

She was my driver; how will I live without her? How will her children live without their mom? How will they know how amazing she was? I will tell them, for the rest of their lives I will tell them.

***

I have decided to start a program in honor of my sister. I have to do something positive, or I will go crazy. I found that while she was sick the one thing that made her feel better was having something to look forward to doing. Her bucket-list items, the next big adventure. No matter how sick she was, we would always go. She even went to the beach five days before she died. On that note, I want to help people live out their bucket list. I will take cancer patients and survivors kayaking. It is the one thing that I know how to do that can benefit others. I have the kayaks and the gear. It will be an honor to do this for her.

When I tell her children about it, they are very willing to help. I am sure that they feel as lost as I do, and this will allow her legacy to live on. Every time I take someone kayaking, I can tell her story, and hopefully help others live their lives to the fullest. I know that Christina would approve.

We decide to call it, "Waters of Hope" and make the logo a kayak, water and a butterfly. I believe it accurately depicts what I want it to represent.

***

My new grandson was born. He came quickly, and I suspect this will be his personality. Eva had him natural because there was no time for an epidural. She was only at the hospital a few hours when he came into the world. Eva hemorrhaged after he was born, and for a brief moment, I thought she would die. My friend is a midwife, and she saved her. It was one of the most terrifying moments of my life. I prayed and begged God for her life. She was fine within hours, but she remained pale for days. It was a reminder to me how fragile life is and how quickly it can be taken from us. As if I needed the lesson.

I love being a grandmother, or a YaYa, which is what they call me. My granddaughter gave me the name, and it fits my personality. It is one of the pure joys of life. It just makes me happy. Life is short, and precious, and having children to watch grow up, eases the pain of loss. It does not dissolve the pain, but it gives it a buffer. I know that Derrick will die soon. I want to deny it, and I will up until the moment when it happens. In my heart, I keep thinking that God will not allow me to lose three siblings. He cannot be that cruel. It would not be fair. But if life has taught me one thing for certain, it is that it is not always fair, and sometimes I cannot save someone, no matter how much I want to save him or her.

CHAPTER 23
Derrick

The End

I HAVE SPENT the last week in the hospital, and I know I am going to die. I want to go home because I know there is nothing else they can do for me. I have lost this battle, and I am tired. In a way, I have been tired of living for some time now. If not for my mom and my family, I would have given up long ago. I have lived for them for a long time. Now I will do the one thing I have wanted to do, and it is to give up. Most people will not understand, and I know that it is selfish. I just cannot do it anymore. My soul is weary.

Mom wants me to go back to Chapel Hill, but they will not take me again. They told me last time it was my last chance. I barely survived that time. I cannot make the trip again and put my body through the healing and then the crash. At this point, my body rejects food even when I attempt to eat. It has given up as well. Mom is struggling with the thought that there is not another option for me. Even if there were, I would not take it. I hate to tell her this, and I hope she sees it on her own. She has done everything she can for me. More than I deserve if I am being honest. She has always been my champion and my defender, even when I am wrong. It is time for her and Sara to let me go. I can tell that Sara is in denial. It is her personality. The Queen of Wishful Thinking. She is stubborn and will refuse to accept things until she does not have a choice. It is her way, but I know when all is said and done, she is strong and will survive. So will Mom.

At this point, I know that I will go home to die. I do not want to die at the hospital. It is too cold and clinical. It is the clinicians' job to try and save me. I want them to let me go, but I will have to go home to do that. They are going to get Hospice for me, so I will have a measure of comfort. Hospice has a different approach to the dying process. They will not try and prolong my life, if that is what I want. They will allow me to die with dignity, and as quickly as possible. It is what I want, and probably the last decision I will make for myself. The decision to die is not an easy one. However, for me it is an easier decision to die than to live. There is a power in letting go.

It makes me sad that I will not watch Jade and Knox grow up. They have become the light of my life. I am so thrilled that I was able to spend time with Jade, and she loves me. I hope she remembers me, and more importantly, I hope she knows that I loved her with my entire heart. I know that I will miss seeing Sara publish her book. She is going to make it happen. She is determined, and she always gets her way in the end.

I know that it will break Mom, and she has already lost one son. Knowing that I have caused her pain, hurts me the most. She is my person. The guilt is strong, but I do not have the ability to fight any longer. My life is over. I am done with trying to live.

Sara thinks she can will me to live by sheer stubbornness. I will not be the one to tell her that she will not get her way in this. I saw her be the same way with Christina. She did not accept it until it happened. Then she was angry and hurt. But she also did what she needed to do and took care of Christina's children. I know that she will do the same thing for Mom. She will make sure that she will be all right. This gives me a degree of comfort.

I see it in Sara's eyes when she talks to me. Mom understands and accepts, but Sara still has to fight. Her never-give-up attitude will not help her this time. The truth is *I* have given up, and she can't make me want to live any longer. The food that I had to make myself throw up in the past comes up now on its own. My body has decided to reject food as my mind did long ago. Doctors could do a feeding tube, but I would find a way to remove it. They cannot force me to live; they cannot force nutrition into my body.

Mom picks me up at the local hospital, and I need assistance getting into the car. The least bit of activity wears me out. When I get home, Sara has to practically carry me into the house. I am past the point where assistance bothers me. I have accepted my fate. I had visitors throughout the day. I am sure some were saying goodbye, and some were trying to make amends. When someone stops by who has mistreated me, I worry that Sara will punch him. The thought makes me chuckle quietly. I can see her doing it, and the only thing that holds her back is Mom. She will not do anything to make things harder on Mom. My father made his appearance and cried the appropriate tears. I allowed him his goodbye, but both of us know the time for amends is long gone. If I were stronger, physically and mentally, I would tell him where to go. My weakness allows him to get what he needs from me; it will be my last gift to him. A gift he did not deserve. Sara looks at him like she wants to murder him, and I know that she will speak her mind to him eventually. It is not in her to hold back her feelings for long.

When everyone leaves, Sara climbs in the bed with me and cries. It is not like her to share her pain with me . . . or with anyone. I allow her to grieve; I allow her to cry and hold me. I know that she needs this, and it is the one thing I can give her. When she has cried all her tears, she apologizes. I want to tell her it is all right, but I am too weak to say the words. Instead I squeeze her hand. It makes her smile, so it is enough.

My mom and I share a bond, and she does not need to hold me or cry. She has already cried her tears. Now there is just acceptance, and even though I will never understand why, guilt. She feels that she could have done something differently. The truth is she went above and beyond what anyone would have done. Most people would have given up on me long ago, and she did not. She has always been my biggest supporter and confidante. She is my person, and I never want her to feel like this was her fault. There is enough blame to go around; she does not need to take any of it. I love her and that love, has made me fight much longer than I wanted to fight. If I can leave her with anything, I want her to know she was my sunshine in the midst of every storm. This was not her fault—none of it was. She is innocent in this. I know that Sara will reiterate this to her, I hope she believes her and remembers that I have said the same thing.

When someone is dying, the person is torn between two worlds, death that is coming, and the life that could have been experienced. I think of all the things I wanted to do. All the places I wanted to go. The people I could have loved, the peace that I so desperately wanted. All of it will elude me. I will wish all these things for the people I love. I want them to live each moment as though it is their last.

Hospice came in. They want to take me to their facility. They can give me better medications, and I know Mom does not want me to die here. It would be too hard for her. I hear their whispers, but I cannot participate in the discussion. The paramedics come and get me. I am too weak for anyone to drive me, and I need constant medication to keep me out of pain. I am starving to death. I no longer feel the hunger pains; those are long gone. However, other things have started to hurt, probably because they are shutting down, and the medication helps with that pain. I know that I should feel more anxiety, but I do not, just acceptance.

At the Hospice center, I can hear all the visitors come in and out. But I cannot respond. Mom and Sara are a continuous presence. Eva and Sean are there as well and my grandmother. I wish I could say a million things to them but I cannot. I guess it is too late for words. I can feel myself fading, and it is impossible to fight any longer. I hope they know I love them and I am sorry for so many things. I know that they love me. That thought brings me comfort and gives me the strength I need to finally let go.

Chapter 24
Sara

Acceptance

DERRICK IS DYING and there is nothing I can do about it. He weighs around sixty pounds, and he is starving to death. They allowed him to come home from the hospital, and we have Hospice called. I know he is really sick because he did not argue about Hospice coming to take care of him. Normally, he is a very private person and does not want anyone but Mom to care for him. However, now he just lets them give him the medication and the care to keep him comfortable.

I crawled in the bed with him and just held him as tightly as I could. He allowed me to be there and allowed me to touch him. I told him that I loved him forever and felt he whispered to me that he was scared. His voice cracked from the effort to try to say words, and at that moment, I wished I could do everything over. There were so many things that I would change. The thought of his simple words broke me into a million pieces. I just held him and cried. He cuddled into me, and we lay there for a long time.

The fact that he was scared increased my sorrow. He had wanted to die for so long that I never thought he would be afraid. He would do things differently as well. This concept made things even sadder than they were before. It was one thing for me to want to do things differently but quite another for him to want to do things over. Why can we see things so clearly when it is too late? Why did we have to get here to see that he could have been saved? There are no answers, only more questions. I know that I will forever drive myself crazy with "what ifs."

When the Hospice workers came this time, they said it would not be long. My time for denial is over. Even with all the knowledge that I have, all the logic from the professionals, the visual of my brother emaciated, I am still in a state of hopefulness that he will survive. I believe in miracles. My brain will not allow me to give up. Christina always told me that it takes me forever to accept things, and she is right. I cannot give up. However, decisions have to be made, and I have to do what everyone wants even if I have to keep the faith. Mom is sad, and I will do what she wants. It is her choice as to where he goes.

After much discussion, it was decided we did not want him to die at home. There were many reasons for this decision, but the main ones were that it would be hard for Mom to deal with living where he had passed away and they could give him better medications at the facility. It was the least we could do for him. I wanted his death, unlike his life, to be peaceful.

Our extended family met us at the facility. They all wanted to say their goodbyes. They gave comfort and support. Their presence filled me with love. It is encouraging when we are hurting to be surrounded by those we love, and those who love us. There is an abundance of love in our family. That love has borne me through hard times, and I know that whatever happens, I will survive, in part, because of that love.

Derrick slipped away peacefully, surrounded by those who loved him the most. I felt so many emotions all at once. Even though I had been expecting his death, when it happened, I felt someone had crushed my heart. Heartbreak is real. The heart actually hurts when it is broken.

I drove Mom home, and she wanted me to do the obituary immediately. I wrote it through a haze of tears. I wanted to encompass his life and his spirit with my words. There are times people do their best work when they are hurting. I felt the words that I wrote would have made Derrick proud. I needed it to represent him. Sometimes words are hard to find. However, that day they flowed from me. Writing has always been an outlet for me—to put my feelings on paper. This skill benefitted me this day, and when I finished, I felt I had accurately described his life and his death. Mom read it and did not want to change anything. She was amazingly calm, but I know enough of grief to know that the pain will come later. It usually shows up after everyone leaves and the bereaved are all alone with their thoughts. I think it is better to feel it and allow it to hurt; at least then, the grief gets out.

The funeral was at our church. Mom planned most of it. I could not concentrate on the words the minister said. All I could think was, *Derrick is dead.* He was never coming back. I could not save him, even though I tried. I never believed he would die. I believed that he would pull through right up until the end. I had lost two siblings. I never believed I would lose three.

At the graveside service, my eyes locked on one of the individuals who had bullied Derrick. A part of me wanted to go over and punch him in the face and another wanted to lecture him and make him hurt the way I was hurting. Instead, I looked him directly in the eye, and I cried. I maintained eye contact while I sobbed. I wanted to pour my pain into him. I wanted him to feel every tear. I wanted him to be sorry. I wanted him to teach his children differently. He held my gaze and shed tears of his own. I had to believe that he was sorry, that he would change things if he could. I turned away and followed my broken family to the grave. It was there that I said my final goodbye to my smart, funny, eccentric little brother.

Epilogue

How could Derrick die, when he never really was able to live? It seems so unfair. With my sister it had been different. She lived every second. But with Derrick, he lived a life of fear, and it breaks me to think about it. I try not to think of all that he could have given to this world. He was quiet and funny. He was an artist, and he loved to make cards for everyone. Who will remember that now?

Who will remember the child who ran through the doctor's office naked? The boy who loved to paint and draw? My defender, even when I was wrong? It does not seem enough that only I will remember. I want everyone to know that he lived. I want them to know that he hurt and had his heart broken. I want people to know that he had an eating disorder but that he tried so hard to overcome it in his own way. He did not try and get better for himself, he wanted to get better for Mom and for me. He wanted to watch Jade and Knox grow up.

He just could not fight anymore, and I was tired of begging him to live. It all makes me very sad.

His bullies get to live and have families. They get to go on vacations and have holidays with their parents. They get to have jobs and all the perks that adulthood brings. They will never know that their actions killed my brother. They are oblivious to all the pain they caused. I wonder sometimes if they would feel guilt, or if the adult versions of them are just as narcissistic and mean as the teenage versions. The only comfort I have is that life has a way of evening the score. One cannot treat nice people badly and get by with it indefinitely. I just wonder if when the karma train hits, will they remember my brother?

I want to find them all and tell them what they have done, and explain to all that they killed my brother. However, I do not trust myself with them . . . and what can they really say that will ease the pain? Sorry is not always enough, and that is really all that they can give me at this point. I had a friend whom I would teasingly tell sometimes, "Sorry doesn't cut it." This is one of those times.

***

I will tell you about my brother. I will tell you so you will remember him. Maybe you will tell someone too. His story, my story might inspire someone. Perhaps, it will make you see bullying as more than just something that children do when they are young. If it makes one person stand up, then all my words are worth the effort. Be gentle. Be kind. Live each day like it is your last because one day it will be. When you leave this world, at least try to leave it better than it was. Live for my brother. He never had the chance. At least now he gets to be the one thing he always wanted. He gets to be invisible.

www.ingramcontent.com/pod-product-compliance
Lightning Source LLC
Chambersburg PA
CBHW070549050426
42450CB00011B/2779